THE
Rebirthing
OF
GOD

Christianity's Struggle for New Beginnings

JOHN PHILIP NEWELL

CHRISTIAN JOURNEYS
FROM SKYLIGHT PATHS® PUBLISHING
Woodstock, Vermont

The Rebirthing of God:
Christianity's Struggle for New Beginnings
2015 Hardcover Edition, Third Printing

Grateful acknowledgment is given for permission to use: THE SUN from *New and Selected Poems, Vol. 1* by Mary Oliver, published by Beacon Press, Boston, Copyright © 1992 by Mary Oliver; PRAYING and WHEN I AM AMONG THE TREES from *Thirst* by Mary Oliver, published by Beacon Press, Copyright © 2006 by Mary Oliver. Used herewith by permission of the Charlotte Sheedy Literary Agency, Inc.

Unless otherwise noted, scripture quotations are from the *New Revised Standard Version Bible*, copyright © 1989 by the Division of Christian Education of the National Council of the Churches of Christ in the USA. Used by permission. All rights reserved.

Library of Congress Cataloging-in-Publication Data
Newell, J. Philip.
The rebirthing of God : Christianity's struggle for new beginnings / John Philip Newell.
pages cm
Includes bibliographical references and index.
ISBN 978-1-59473-542-4 (alk. paper) — ISBN 978-1-59473-574-5 (ebook)
1. Christianity—21st century. I. Title.
BR121.3.N53 2014
230—dc23

2014027850

10 9 8 7 6 5 4 3
Manufactured in the United States of America
Jacket Design: Jenny Buono
Cover Photograph: Margaret Woodsen Nea; "Iona Dawn 2013"; mkwphotography1@gmail.com.
Interior Design: Tim Holtz

SkyLight Paths is creating a place where people of different spiritual traditions come together for challenge and inspiration, a place where we can help each other understand the mystery that lies at the heart of our existence.

SkyLight Paths sees both believers and seekers as a community that increasingly transcends traditional boundaries of religion and denomination—people wanting to learn from each other, *walking together, finding the way.*

SkyLight Paths, "Walking Together, Finding the Way," and colophon are trademarks of LongHill Partners, Inc., registered in the U.S. Patent and Trademark Office.
Walking Together, Finding the Way®
Published by SkyLight Paths Publishing
A Division of LongHill Partners, Inc.
Sunset Farm Offices, Route 4, P.O. Box 237
Woodstock, VT 05091
Tel: (802) 457-4000   Fax: (802) 457-4004
www.skylightpaths.com

To
Peregrini Christi
and their journey into love

Contents

Chapter 4:
RECONNECTING WITH THE JOURNEY

Journeying into Unknown Territory

Traveling as Pilgrims

Shedding Our Attachment to the Ego

Finding the Other Half of Our Soul

Chapter 5:
RECONNECTING WITH SPIRITUAL PRACTICE

A Contemplative Orientation

Finding Our Diamond Essence

Plunging Deep into the Heart of the World

Nurturing the Seed-Force for Change

Chapter 6:
RECONNECTING WITH NONVIOLENCE

Response-Ability

Love-Force Not Brute-Force

Love Is the Strongest Yet Humblest Force

Blessed Are the Peacemakers

Chapter 7:
RECONNECTING WITH THE UNCONSCIOUS

Opening to the Well of the Imagination

The Marriage of the Conscious and the Unconscious

The Promise of Union

Dreaming the Way Forward

Introduction

I am writing this book on the isle of Iona. Or, more exactly, in my imagination I am on Iona as I write this book. Legend has it that this little island in the Hebrides was the birthplace of Christianity for Scotland in the sixth century. It was a place of new beginnings for a whole nation and for many people well beyond the bounds of this land. Since then it has been a place of pilgrimage to which tens of thousands come from the four corners of the earth every year seeking new birth. They come longing for healing for themselves and for their families. They come searching for signs of a way forward for their cherished homelands and for the one home to which we all belong, the earth.

So this is a good place to write about rebirthing. It has witnessed the spiritual birth throes of many before us and it will witness them again, if we come seeking. In *The Rebirthing of God: Christianity's Struggle for New Beginnings*, I invite us to imagine what new birth would look like in our lives individually and collectively. Specifically, I invite those of us who belong to the Christian household—whether in its well-defined bounds of practice and belief or on its disenchanted edges of inheritance and doubt—to dream together of a reborn Christianity that might again carry great blessing for the world and usher in the emergence of a new well-being for the earth.

Julian of Norwich, the fourteenth-century Christian mystic, said most simply but most radically that we are not just made by God, we are made of God.[1] We are not just fashioned from afar by a distant Creator. We are born from the very womb of the Divine. This is why Julian so loves to refer to God as Mother as well as Father. She sees us as coming forth from the essence of the One who is the Source of all things.

What does it mean that we are made *of* God rather than simply *by* God? In part it means that the wisdom of God is deep within us, deeper than the ignorance of what we have done. It is to say that the creativity of God is deep within us, deeper than any barrenness in our lives or relationships, deeper than any endings in our families or our world. Within us—as a sheer gift of God—is the capacity to bring forth what has never been before, including what has never been imagined before. Above all else, as Julian says, the love-longings of God are at the heart of our being.[2] We and all things have come forth from the One. Deep within us are holy, natural longings for oneness, primal sacred drives for union. We may live in tragic exile from these longings, or we may have spent a whole lifetime not knowing how to truly satisfy them, but they are there at the heart of our being, waiting to be born afresh.

In St. John's Gospel, Jesus speaks of the need to be "born anew" (John 3:7). This phrase, more familiarly rendered as "born again," has been hijacked by religious fundamentalism to give the impression that we need to become something other than ourselves. The phrase has been applied so often to preach a turning from what is deepest within us and a denial of our human nature that many in the Christian household understandably have recoiled from its use. But the phrase needs to be reclaimed. It is close to the heart of Jesus's teachings and points to the necessity of what is deepest in us coming forth again. Its urgency speaks of what is at the heart of all things—made of God—being set free to emerge in radically new ways. *The Rebirthing of God* is precisely this. It is pointing to a radical reemergence of the Divine from deep within us. We do not have to create it. We cannot create it. But we can let it spring forth and be reborn in our lives. We can be part of midwifing new holy births in the world.

One of the great prophets of the modern human soul was Carl Jung (1875–1961), the founder of analytical psychology. Even as a boy he had prophetic intuitions, although for many of these he did not find language, or the courage to speak, until many decades later in his life. As a twelve-year-old boy in Switzerland, walking home from school one day past Basel Cathedral with its shining new spire, the young Carl Jung became aware of an image rising up from the unconscious. He was so horrified by it that he tried pushing it back down. But it kept insisting on coming forth. When finally, as he explained years later, he allowed himself to name what he was seeing, he saw that above the spire of the cathedral was the throne of God. Descending from the throne was "an enormous turd" that smashed into the spire and the walls of the cathedral crumbled.[3]

We are living in the midst of the great turd falling. In fact, it has already hit the spire, and the walls of Western Christianity are collapsing. In many parts of the West that collapse can only be described as seismic. In another twenty-five years, much of the Western Christian household, as we have known it, will be no more. One only has to look around on a typical Sunday in most of our mainstream Christian churches. Who will be there in another quarter of a century?

There are three main responses or reactions to this collapse. The first is to deny that it is happening. The second is to frantically try to shore up the foundations of the old thing. The third, which I invite us into, is to ask what is trying to be born that requires a radical reorientation of our vision. What is the new thing that is trying to emerge from deep within us and from deep within the collective soul of Christianity?

A few years ago after sharing Jung's dreamlike awareness of the enormous turd at a spirituality conference in the United States, a woman came up to me at the end of my talk. She explained that she was a midwife and that in her twenty-five years of midwifery she had noticed that the turd nearly always comes before the birth. In other words, what is it that we need to let go of to prepare the way for new birthing?

Here on Iona I find myself in the Abbey Church on a Sunday morning. It is full. There are people from many nations. I would say that most of them have come as pilgrims, that is, as seekers of new beginnings, whether they be guests and volunteers at the Abbey, longer-term staff, day visitors to the island, retreatants making longer pilgrimage, or islanders in from their crofts and crafts. We are here to pray together for new beginnings. But when I look around, I realize that here, too, the vast majority are white-haired. Great yearnings may have brought us to this place, but again the gathering speaks of the end of an era.

The liturgy is being led by women, able and articulate, but where are the men? When it comes time for the bread and wine to be carried in procession to the high altar for communion, again on this occasion it is all women carrying the elements, the exact reverse of the tragic imbalance of male domination that has plagued the Christian household for centuries. In the past this disparity would have bothered me. Why could a man or two not have been found to take part? But on this occasion something else begins to stir in my heart. Instead of seeing it as a communion procession, I begin to experience it as a funeral procession. Instead of bread and wine being carried forward for the sacrament, it becomes in my soul's eye the Church as body of Christ being borne for burial. The vision is both beautiful and sorrowful. I weep as I watch. Such poignant beauty. The women have not fled at the death. They are faithfully tending the body with care, with reverence. And such huge sorrow. This is death. This form will be no more.

We are at such a moment. We are being asked not to flee in the face of the death of Christianity as we have known it. It is not just women who are being asked to be strong. It is that feminine depth of faithfulness in us all that is being asked to be true. Not that we are to judge the vast majority who have fled in order to find nourishment elsewhere. Responsibility for this is with the entire household, not merely with the individuals who no longer come to the family table. They are not coming because they have not been fed. They have not been given the spiritual fare to nourish them for this moment in time. Much of what is happening within the four walls of our household—liturgically, theologically, spiritually—is irrelevant to the great journey of the earth today and of humanity's most pressing struggles. Nevertheless, we are being asked not to flee. But in staying, both reverently and sorrowfully, we are not being asked to deny that the death is occurring or to defend the irrelevance and sometimes falseness that have led to the collapse.

Recently, I was in Ireland with the Sisters of the Presentation of the Blessed Virgin Mary, known colloquially as the Presentation Sisters. They deeply impressed me with their radical faithfulness. They do not pretend that all is well in their Church. Even their own order is experiencing devastating numerical decline. But in the midst of this awareness of death, they focus not on the perpetuity of their own community but on how they can faithfully serve the Spirit of new birth in the world now. They bring their wisdom, their lands, and their vocations to something infinitely larger than the religious form they have inherited. Yes, they tend its dying expressions with reverence, and indeed at times with sorrow, but they do not hesitate to speak against the abuses of power that have given shelter to wrongdoing and made their Church irrelevant. Ecclesiastical authority does not intimidate them. They simply get on with following their holy instinct for oneness with the poor, oneness with the wisdom of other traditions, and, increasingly, oneness with the earth in its yearnings for healing. In County Cork in the southwest of Ireland, I found that they had turned over the farming of their land to young Irish men and women to organically tend it. On that same land, instead of the traditional stations of the cross, there is a stations of the cosmos walk, inseparably linking their life of contemplation and action with the great journey of the universe. We may not yet know what this faithful letting go will mean for the future of the Presentation Sisters in Ireland, and the many similar expressions of faithfulness in women's religious orders throughout the Western world. But we can know that such faith—such faithful letting go—will bear fruit.

Carl Jung observed that in the Christian resurrection story the risen Christ is not found where his body was laid. The story is not about resuscitation. It is about resurrection. It is not about reviving the old form. It is about something new, something we could never have imagined, emerging from death. This is the way of the universe, made of God. It is forever finding its new form, forever unfolding into what has never been before. This is the way of our souls, our lives, our communities—all made of God. The invitation is to let go to the flow of the

One deep within us, this mighty subterranean river of God that courses through all things.

Where is this river of God taking us in our lives and relationships today? More specifically, what are the features of new beginnings for our religious household? We are so deeply immersed in collapse, as well as the early stirrings of new birth, that it is difficult to sharply define the characteristics of the new thing that is trying to emerge. But there are some clear intimations of what the rebirthing might look like and there are some modern prophets, both Christian and other faiths, who are clearly pointing the way.

Chapter 1, "Reconnecting with the Earth," focuses on one of the primary features of the rebirthing, namely a coming back into relationship with the sacredness of the earth. As the eco-theologian Thomas Berry puts it, "We need to move from a spirituality of alienation from the natural world to a spirituality of intimacy with the natural world."[4] Everything in the universe is related to everything else in the universe. We will do well not to pretend that we can look after ourselves in isolation but to know that the earth's well-being is an essential part of our well-being.

Chapter 2, "Reconnecting with Compassion," looks at the threefold way of compassion as a key to rebirthing—the courage to see, the courage to feel, and the courage to act. Individually and collectively, we will carry blessing for the world when we live compassionately. This, as Aung San Suu Kyi, the leader of the nonviolent movement for democracy in Burma says, is living the full life.[5] We will be truly alive, she says, not by focusing solely on our own needs—whether as individuals, nations, or a species—but by choosing to bear responsibility for the needs of all humanity.

Chapter 3, "Reconnecting with the Light," explores the important discipline of looking for light at the heart of all life. The light of God is not simply a feature of the universe. It is the essence of the universe. If this light were somehow extracted from the body of the cosmos, everything would cease to exist. This, says the Pulitzer Prize–winning poet Mary Oliver, is why we "have come into the world ... to be filled with light, and to shine."[6] The Sacred will be reborn within us and among us when we remember, again and again, the light, naming it at the heart of one another and knowing that we carry it for one another.

Chapter 4, "Reconnecting with the Journey," looks at the necessity of traveling into territory well beyond the bounds of our own religious inheritance. The great English Benedictine Bede Griffiths calls it finding the other half of our soul.[7] Humanity's great wisdom traditions are given not to compete with each other but to complete each other. We need each other as much as the species of the earth need one another to be whole. Rebirthing will happen within our Christian household when we reverently approach the heart of other traditions. It is what Griffiths in his work in India calls the "marriage of East and West," a conjoining of what has been tragically torn apart.[8]

Chapter 5, "Reconnecting with Spiritual Practice," focuses on contemplative practice and meditation as essential features of the rebirthing. Whether in our relationship with nature or in the varied disciplines of mindfulness, there is a growing desire for an experience *of* the Sacred rather than simply belief *about* the Sacred. In meditative awareness, says the American Trappist monk Thomas Merton, we penetrate "the inmost ground" of our being.[9] In contemplative practice we experience God in ways that enable us to be aware of God in the whole of life. This is where we will find true strength for the holy work of transformation in the world.

Chapter 6, "Reconnecting with Nonviolence," considers what Mahatma Gandhi (1869–1948), the father of Indian independence, called "soul-force." In his view, this is the opposite of brute-force, and soul-force is the primary energy for bringing about real and sustainable change and resolving our conflicts as nations and communities.[10] The parallel to this in the Christian household is radically reclaiming the nonviolence of Jesus's teachings as an essential feature of rebirthing. As Gandhi said, if Christians had actually done what Jesus taught us to do—namely, love our enemy—the world would long ago have been transformed.

Chapter 7, "Reconnecting with the Unconscious," looks at how we are to dream the way forward. Whether in our individual lives or together as communities and religious traditions, if there is to be new birth, we need to access depths of knowing that the rational mind on its own cannot reach. As Carl Jung says, wellness is found through an integration of the unconscious into consciousness.[11] Rebirthing will be served by opening again to the well of wisdom that flows deep in the world of dream life, intuition, and humanity's collective inheritance of myth and legend.

Chapter 8, "Reconnecting with Love," leads us into the sine qua non of rebirthing. Love is the pure origin of desire, the true source of conception, the fertile beginnings of new birth. When we love, we bring the very essence of our being into relationship with the essence of the other. God in us adores God in the other. As the French philosopher Simone Weil says, it is our "nuptial yes," our commitment to be one.[12] We are created for love. There is no other energy that can truly bring together, individually or collectively, what has been torn apart by fear and hatred. Love frees us from our bondage to the ego. It awakens us to the holy desire for justice. Love is pregnant with hope. Without it there can be no rebirth.

Each chapter of this book focuses on one particular station of pilgrimage on Iona as a metaphor of new beginnings. We begin, as our Iona pilgrimages always do, in the thirteenth-century Nunnery that sits open to the elements. There we reflect on the need to come back into relationship with the earth. We then make our way to the Crossroads where the north-south road intersects with the east-west road. There we ask what will guide us at the great crossroads of our lives, remembering especially the way of compassion. Next is the Hill of the Angels where we celebrate the shafts of Divine Light that can be glimpsed in all things. Then it is on to St. Columba's Bay, where we remember Columba's journey in the sixth century from his homeland to discover new beginnings. There we reflect on our own journeys, especially into the unknown territory of other wisdom traditions. We then head to the Hermit's Cell at the heart of the island to consider the role of spiritual practice in rebirthing the Sacred. After that we ascend to the highest point on the island, Dun I, from which we cast our eyes over life's most conflicted places, recommitting ourselves to the way of nonviolence. Then we encounter the Well of Eternal Youth on our descent. We gaze into its waters to remember the depths of the unconscious from which dreams for new beginnings can emerge. And finally we stand in a circle around St. Martin's Cross in front of the Abbey. There we pledge ourselves again to love as the only force that can bring together what has been torn apart in our lives and our world.

It was on Iona years ago that I first became aware of the need to reclaim some of the features of ancient Christianity in the Celtic world as lost treasure for today. Part of that treasure is the much-cherished image of John the Evangelist, also known as John the Beloved, leaning against Jesus at the Last Supper. Celtic tradition holds that by doing this he heard the heartbeat of God. He became a symbol of the practice of listening—listening deep within ourselves, within one another, and within the body of the earth for the beat of the Sacred Presence.[13]

Do we know that within each one of us is the unspeakably beautiful beat of the Sacred? Do we know that we can honor that Sacredness in one another and in everything that has being? And do we know that this combination—growing in awareness that we are bearers of Presence, along with a faithful commitment to honor that Presence in one another and in the earth—holds the key to transformation in our world?

Throughout this book, as we reflect together on the rebirthing of God, I invite us to return to this essential posture of spirituality, listening for the beat of the Sacred within ourselves and within the body of the earth. To *return*, or to *reconnect* as the chapter titles of this book emphasize, is not to suggest that the answer lies in going back to something that was. The invitation is to recover an inner stance of listening that will equip us to move forward into new beginnings we may not yet even be able to imagine. This is my prayer—that we may grow in such awareness and commitment. Together they hold the promise of rebirth.

Chapter 1

Reconnecting with the Earth

The first thing that is said about humanity in the Hebrew Scriptures is that we are made in the image and likeness of God (Genesis 1:26). Everything else written about us in our scriptural inheritance needs to be read in light of this foundational truth: that within us is the likeness of the One from whom we have come. Or, as Julian of Norwich puts it, we are made "of God."[1] We are made of the Light that was in the beginning. We are made of the Wisdom that fashioned the universe in its glory of interrelatedness. We are made of the Love that longs for oneness. This is not to deny our capacity for falseness and for the ugly betrayals that tear us apart. It is simply to say that deeper still is our of-Godness.

What would it look like for these true depths to fully come forth again? What would this mean in our lives individually, and collectively as members of communities and citizens of nations? And, in particular, what would it look like in our religious traditions, in our Christian household? A primary feature of such rebirthing is the desire to move back into relationship with everything else that is of God. It means choosing to move in harmony with the universe again, knowing the rising of the sun and the whiteness of the moon as part of us, seeing the beauty and wildness of the creatures as expressions of what is also within us, the unnameable and untameable presence of the Divine in all things. It means growing in awareness of earth's sacredness, knowing that its moist greenness issues forth directly from the ever-fresh fecundity of God.[2]

The Cathedral of Earth, Sea, and Sky

On Iona, every time I return, the first place I long to pray is the ruins of the thirteenth-century Nunnery. This is not to belittle the rebuilt Abbey of the same period up the road, a place of prayer that holds fond memories for me. But the deeper stirring of attraction in me is for the Nunnery. I am not alone in this. Increasingly, I find others sharing this sense of holiness—individuals praying in silence or groups celebrating simple ritual and dance together. What is this all about?

The Abbey is enclosed. It has a roof and four strong walls. The Nunnery, on the other hand, is open. It stands free to the elements. There is a yearning within us to come back into relationship with all things. The ancient Celts spoke of the cathedral of earth, sea, and sky. This is the yearning—new and at the same time ancient—that is stirring among us today, to pray again in the living cathedral of the universe.

When my wife and I first arrived on Iona in 1988 to take up leadership at the Abbey, the weekly pilgrimage around the island did not even stop at the Nunnery. It is difficult to believe, but the pilgrimage route walked right past it. Most of the historical focus has been on the rebuilt Abbey. History—which in the Western world has usually implied *his* story—has focused on the life of men in religious community. Her story, on the other hand, the life of women in community, has been almost entirely neglected.

The desire to pray in the Nunnery is the desire to pray again in relationship with the earth. Directly related to this is the desire to come back into relationship with the feminine as sacred. Our religion, like so much of our Western culture, has suffered a tragic imbalance. The neglect and exploitation of the earth have gone hand in hand with a subordination and abuse of the feminine. This has often included a fear of the feminine and its deep birthing energies. Praying in the Nunnery is part of the growing desire in us to bring back into relationship again so-called opposites that have been torn apart, the masculine and the feminine, as well as the life of humanity and the life of the earth.

In New Harmony, Indiana, there is a modern place of prayer that addresses this same yearning. It is called the Roofless Church. It has four defining walls, but there is no roof. Like the Nunnery, it sits open to the elements. It was created under the inspiration of Jane Blaffer Owen (1915–2010), one of the most beautiful and wise women I have ever known. Over fifty years ago, well in advance of today's earth awareness movement, Jane Owen saw that our sacred sites must not be represented by separation from the elements. Our holy gathering spaces must not be characterized by division from the creatures and from earth's other peoples and religious traditions.

> A primary feature of such rebirthing is the desire to move back into relationship with everything else that is of God.

At the heart of the Roofless Church is a sculpture by the Jewish artist Jacques Lipchitz (1891–1973). It is called *The Descent of the Spirit.* In the form of a dove the Spirit descends onto an abstract divine feminine form that opens to give birth. At one level Lipchitz is pointing to the Jesus story, conceived by the Spirit in the womb of Mary. At another level he is pointing to the universe story. Everything is conceived by the Spirit in the womb of the cosmos. Everything is sacred.

Jane Owen met Lipchitz in New York City at the end of the Second World War through the German-American theologian Paul Tillich (1886–1965). Lipchitz had escaped Nazi-occupied France with the help of a Roman Catholic priest in Plateau d'Assy. Even before his escape, he had conceived the idea of this sculpture. In New York he shared his vision with Jane Owen. She commissioned him to create three casts of the piece. One was to be in the Roofless Church of New Harmony. The second was to be in the parish church of Assy in France. The third was to be in the National Cathedral in Washington, D.C.

The cathedral leaders agreed in principle to feature the sculpture, but when they saw it, they refused to accept it. It was too explicit in its representation of the Divine Feminine opening to give birth. So instead, as Jane Owen explained to me when I met her many years later, they commissioned another artist to create a statue of George Washington riding a horse! The young Jane Owen was upset by their refusal. She went to New York to pour out her soul to a religious sister who told her there was someone visiting from Scotland whom she should meet. His name was George MacLeod (1895–1991). He and his young Scottish community were in the midst of rebuilding Iona Abbey.

I would have loved to be there for that first meeting. Jane Owen was as formidable a feminine presence as George MacLeod was a masculine energy. They later became good friends, but on that first occasion they had only a few minutes together. Jane said to George, "The third cast belongs on Iona." To which George replied, "We Presbyterians would find it difficult to live with a sculpture of Our Lady, but if she were to arrive with a dowry we would find it easier to live with her." So she arrived with a dowry, and that dowry paid for the rebuilding of the cloisters of Iona Abbey.

George MacLeod was right, of course. Scottish Presbyterians would not find it easy to live with a sculpture of Our Lady, and especially its explicitly feminine birthing form. Nor would they find it easy to live with Lipchitz's name for the piece, *Our Lady of Delight*. They might not know what to do with the Divine Feminine, but they also would not know what to do with delight! So MacLeod renamed the sculpture *The Descent of the Spirit*, and there she sits in the cloisters of Iona Abbey. Every time I see her I feel that her time has come. More and more it can be said that she belongs to this moment in time. She represents the recovery of the feminine that we are in the midst of, and with the feminine a recovery of the awareness that everything that is born is sacred.

Whether it is in the Nunnery on Iona or the Roofless Church of New Harmony, the time has come for us to make the connection again between spirituality and the earth. We may not all literally be able to gather together to pray in open spaces like the Nunnery or the Roofless Church. But wherever our sacred sites are, we must ensure that the language we use, the rituals we celebrate, and the symbols we employ keep pointing to the great living cathedral of earth, sea, and sky. At best, our so-called sacred sites are like side chapels that need to open onto the living sanctuary of the universe.

One of the things I love to do on Iona—and I notice almost everyone else doing it as well—is to study the stones on the beaches, to handle their sea-smoothed roundness, to notice the veins of different colors intermingled, each stone absolutely unique. Iona has some of the most ancient geological formations in the world, right at its surface, immediately accessible to sight and touch. So, the type of stone I especially look for on Iona is the island's most ancient rock, Lewisian Gneiss. It is 2.8 billion years old.

It is difficult to know exactly what this number means. But one way to understand it is to say that these stones are two-thirds the age of the earth or one-quarter the age of the Milky Way, this great galaxy to which we belong. A hundred years ago we thought this was all there was to the universe. What we now know is that there are billions of galaxies, each with billions of stars. It just keeps unfolding!

Everything that has emerged in space and time has come forth from a tiny pinprick of light that exploded the universe into being 13.8 billion years ago. As the physicist David Bohm put it in his seminal work *Wholeness and the Implicate Order*, everything is like an explication of what was implicated in that first moment.[3] Everything that has unfolded in space and time was present in utero in the universe's beginnings, so interrelated are we and all things with that initial flaring forth of light.

The Whole Universe Takes Part in the Dance

Teachers in the Celtic world have been saying something similar for a long time. In the ninth century, John Scotus Eriugena said that all things in the universe were made "together and at once."[4] He did not mean that we and all things became visible at the same time. He meant that we and all things have been hidden in the "secret folds of nature," as he put it, waiting for the time of our manifestation.[5] We have been latent in the matter of the universe since its inception. Now is the time of our emergence.

Bohm describes reality as "undivided wholeness in flowing movement."[6] The universe is like a mighty river in flow. From that single stream, smaller streams emerge. These are to be celebrated and cherished, each one absolutely unique, never to be repeated again—that blade of grass, that autumn leaf, the countenance of that child, your life, my life. Then we dissolve, merging back into the flow, our constituent parts to emerge again in new formations further down the river. The universe wastes nothing in its endless unfolding.

Within that flow everything is interrelated. There is a propensity within all things to move in relationship, even though we may choose to deny that predisposition or be untrue to it. The law of gravitation expresses it. At some level every atom in the universe seeks to remain in relationship with every other atom. Science observes this propensity without claiming to understand it. Brian Swimme (b. 1950), an evolutionary cosmologist, calls it the "urge to merge."[7] It is the desire for oneness that was implicit in the universe's beginnings. Everything has a yearning to move in relationship. The earth has been revolving around the sun for 4.5 billion years. This could be described as a long-term stable relationship! It is a love affair. We have been born of that love affair.

> But wherever our sacred sites are, we must ensure that the language we use, the rituals we celebrate, and the symbols we employ keep pointing to the great living cathedral of earth, sea, and sky.

If humanity can be understood as a microcosmos—a miniature of the cosmos—then the cosmos can be described as a macroanthropos—a magnification of humanity. We are not an exception to the cosmos. We are not an addendum. Humanity has emerged from within the matter of the cosmos. We express the nature of the universe. What is deepest in us—our longing for relationship—reveals a yearning that is within all things. Yes, we may be a unique expression of that longing—just as everything else uniquely reveals some aspect of reality—but what we manifest is a yearning that emerges from the very heart of creation.

In the Celtic world there is great fondness for John the Beloved, the one who leaned against Jesus at the Last Supper. As I have already noted, he became an image of listening for the heartbeat of God within all things. This has led me over the years to delve more deeply into the legends and writings attributed to John and his community in Asia Minor in the first century CE. One of these writings is the Acts of John, which includes a beautiful description of the Last Supper and an image of all things moving in relationship.

Jesus invites the disciples to form a circle so that they can conclude the meal with a Hebrew circle dance. At one point in the dance, Jesus stands in the middle and says, "The whole universe takes part in the dancing."[8] He is the memory of what we have forgotten—that everything moves in relationship. He comes to lead us not into a detachment from the earth or a separation from the other species and peoples of the world, but into a dance that will bring us back into relationship with all things. He is pointing to what is deepest in the body of the earth and to what is deepest within each of us—the desire to move in harmony.

Perhaps it is this that makes me so want to touch the 2.8-billion-year-old stones of Iona. They represent something deep within and closer to the origins of the earth than almost anything else we can touch. And maybe this is why we journey in pilgrimage to places like Iona and Jerusalem and Mecca, because we want to get in touch with our beginnings. We want to touch again what is deepest in us and in our traditions and to reconnect with the One who is our source. For in touching the innermost strands of our being, we will be born anew.

I left Iona in 1992 to become the assistant minister at St. Giles Cathedral in Edinburgh. Early in my time at the cathedral I had a dream in which I was in the pulpit about to begin a sermon. Above me in the dream I saw that there was no roof. The sanctuary opened out onto the cosmos. It was like the Roofless Church of New Harmony, although at that time I was not yet familiar with that structure. Below me in the dream was an artificial ceiling. It separated me from the people. They could hear me, but I could not see them. So I had to make a decision. Should I remain in the open place or descend to preach from under the artificial ceiling? I realized that I must speak from the openness, from the place of the relationship with all things.

This is a particular dream that came to me at a particular moment in my life. But it is a dream, I believe, that belongs to all of us and to this moment in time. We are being asked to decide where we shall stand. Will we speak from self-contained places such as communities and religious traditions or will we choose to speak from the open place of relationship with the earth and all its creatures?

At the Heart of Matter Is the Heart of God

The first modern Christian prophet of the sacredness of the universe was Pierre Teilhard de Chardin (1881–1955), a French Jesuit priest and scientist. I use the term *modern* prophet because there have been earlier prophets in the Christian tradition who have clearly articulated the sacredness of all being—Hildegard of Bingen in the twelfth century, for instance, or John Scotus Eriugena in the ninth century, to name but a few. But Teilhard was the first in the modern period to remember what these earlier teachers had known, that "at the heart of matter is the heart of God."[9] The deeper we move into the mystery of any created thing, the closer we come to the Divine Presence. He also believed that what the Christian doctrine of the Incarnation teaches us to see is that "We can be saved only by becoming one with the universe."[10] The story of the incarnate Christ points to the oneness of heaven and earth, the Divine and the human, spirit and matter. It points not to an exclusive truth, but to the most inclusive of truths. It does not limit the sacredness to one man at one moment in time. It reveals the essential sacredness of every person and everything that has been created.

Not surprisingly Teilhard, in propounding the sacredness of the universe, ran into resistance from his ecclesiastical superiors. Such teachings hold radical implications for how we see and treat one another as individuals and nations, and for how we relate to the resources and creatures of the earth. In 1926 the Vatican silenced Teilhard by forbidding him to teach and publish his theological writings. Instead, they sent him to China to take up the post of paleontologist in an archaeological dig. The plan was to get rid of him. Little did his superiors realize, however, what the East would do to Teilhard! In China, as he continued to reflect on the sacredness of the universe, he came to see what he called the "fragrance" of the feminine in all things—that dimension within us and within the matter of the universe that attracts union.[11] Not only is the universe sacred, it holds within itself a magnetism of unity.

Teilhard returned to Europe after the Second World War, but it was not long before he again aroused in his ecclesiastical superiors suspicions of heresy. Once more he was sent into exile from France, this time to the United States. There he was assigned to the Jesuit home in New York City, although often he was away—in Africa and elsewhere—on paleontological pursuits. During these years we can imagine Teilhard literally digging into the ground as he also dug deep into the mystery of the universe in his spiritual search for the Sacred. "The more I give myself to the earth," he said, "the more I belong to God."[12]

Teilhard had been forbidden by the Vatican to publish his spiritual and theological writings. In his desire to be faithful to the Church that he loved, he chose, for the most part, to obey its restrictions. But before he died he engaged in a final act of disobedience. He was persuaded by friends to sign over his writings to the safekeeping of his personal secretary in France, Mademoiselle Jeanne Mortier. This meant that, at death, his writings would belong not to the Church but to her. He died on Easter Day, 1955. His writings would soon burst onto the world.

I still meet Roman Catholic priests today who were training in the late 1950s. They have memories of reading Teilhard's forbidden material at night under the covers by flashlight in their seminary dorms, and of strapping his books under their mattresses by day. This is exactly what theology should be—so exciting, so relevant to the human journey and the unfolding story of the universe, that we will read it no matter who tells us not to!

One of the themes to emerge in the posthumous writings of Teilhard was his belief that Christianity was "reaching the end of one of the natural cycles of its existence."[13] It needed to be "born again."[14] The most prominent feature of a reborn Christianity, he said, was that Christ would be viewed not as a "deserter" of the earth but as a lover of the earth.[15] The "primacy of humility" would be seen as the foremost mark of our Christhood and Christianity's primary blessing to the world—living in relationship to the sacred *humus* of the earth.[16] Oneness with the Divine, Christianity's greatest goal, would be experienced not as a looking away from the earth but as "communion with God through earth."[17] We must "let the very heart of the earth ... beat within us," he wrote.[18]

Perhaps it is John the Beloved who best articulates Christianity's gift for the world when he writes that "you cannot hate your brother or sister and love God" (1 John 4:20; adapted). You cannot do it because they are one. Teilhard's version of this would have been to say that we cannot hate the earth, we cannot neglect or abuse the earth, and claim to love God. We cannot do it because they are one. Not only do we need a new way of seeing, but we also need to forge a new way of living. We must usher in a radical rebirth of our relationship with the earth and its creatures if we are to thrive.

A Spirituality of Intimacy with the Natural World

If Teilhard can be described as the first modern Christian prophet of earth's sacredness, then Thomas Berry (1914–2009), a student of Teilhard's writings, can be described as the first Christian prophet of the protection of the earth. Teilhard *saw* the sacredness. Berry called on us to *protect* it. A theologian and cultural historian by training, Berry preferred to call himself a "geologian."[19] Earth was God's great work, he said, and to serve in that great work is humanity's highest calling.[20]

As a prophet, Berry did not shy away from drawing attention to the "extinction spasm" that we are in the midst of.[21] Over three hundred species a week are becoming extinct, in part because of how we are choosing to live—or, more precisely, because of how we are choosing *not* to live—in relationship with the earth. In the last century we have undone much of what it took the earth four billion years to evolve.

Berry loved the Christian household well enough to criticize it and call on it to change. Responsibility for the degradation of the earth was not to be laid solely at the door of Western Christianity, but he saw clearly that we have been complicit in the crime. The nations at the forefront of our planetary degradation over the last hundred years have been predominantly Christian nations. Given the excessive orientation in our religious inheritance toward transcendence, we have tragically failed to protect the sacredness of the earth. What we now need, he said, is a theology of radical immanence. "We need to move from a spirituality of alienation from the natural world to a spirituality of intimacy with the natural world."[22] And rather than viewing ourselves as separate from the earth, we need always to remember that we are "Earthlings," he said.[23] We do not have the capacity in and by ourselves to save the earth. We do, however, have the capacity to serve the earth and to nurture its deep energies for healing, to allow it the space and the time to renew itself.

The Qur'an includes a beautiful description of the creation of humanity. It describes God as drawing us forth from the dark, moist soil. When the first man and woman have emerged from the fecundity of earth's womb, God instructs the angels to bow down before them. The angels prostrate themselves, with one exception. The greatest angel, Satan, refuses. He says to God, "I will not bow to a human being whom You created from the mud" (Al-Hijr Valley 15:33).

> Berry loved the Christian household well enough to criticize it and call on it to change. Responsibility for the degradation of the earth was not to be laid solely at the door of Western Christianity, but he saw clearly that we have been complicit in the crime.

Is this not the root of our falseness, refusing to bow to the sacredness of what comes forth from the earth? Is this not the pattern in most of our division as nations and as a human species—the refusal to honor what is deepest in others? Satan chooses the way of hubris, of pride, of lifting himself up over the other. Think of the hubris of our nations, our religious traditions, of humanity's arrogance over the earth. It is the beginning of Satan's falseness and it is the heart of our betrayal of one another.

We need to be aware of our failures. This is essential to the way forward. Equally important, we must be aware of our successes. When the Christian household gets it right—that is, when we embody our vision for justice, live our commitment to the poor, move in harmony with the earth—we can get it right like no other entity in the Western world.

A few years ago I was invited to the Cathedral of St. John the Divine in New York City for St. Francis's Sunday. I was staying in the cathedral cloisters and, when I got up early on the Sunday morning to go out for coffee, there on the street in front of me, hours before the service was to begin, were hundreds of people lined up with their dogs, cats, and pets of every description. They were waiting to get into the cathedral for the great celebration of the blessing of the creatures, a liturgy that happens every year on the Sunday closest to St. Francis's feast day on October 2.

The Cathedral was full that day, packed to the gunwales. It is fuller on St. Francis's Sunday than on Christmas or Easter. New Yorkers come there by the thousands—many of them for their one and only day of church attendance all year to celebrate the sacredness of the earth and its creatures.

> We need to be aware of our failures. This is essential to the way forward.

The service overflowed with creativity. Paul Winter, the composer of the *Missa Gaia*, was there. He had woven wolf and whale sounds into the sung liturgy. At one point in the celebration, dancers from a New York contemporary dance troupe leapt in front of the altar and all around it as creatures of earth, sea, and sky. Throughout the service parakeets perched on people's shoulders and magnificent macaws squawked raucously in response to the choir. It all felt like true worship—alive, vibrant with the yearnings of this moment in time, and inclusive of the whole of creation.

Toward the end of the liturgy we moved into what is called the Silent Procession of the Creatures, silent to honor them but also so as not to startle them as they enter. The huge west-facing doors opened and in came the wonderful train of creatures, both large and small, exotic and domestic, wild and tame. Leading the procession was a camel, its long neck reaching forward to look from side to side. One wondered who was on display here! A boa constrictor followed the camel, then a pig, a goat, and the whole spectrum of God's creatures. At times it felt like being on a *Lord of the Rings* film set. I almost expected great trees to come walking down the central aisle. Of course, the cathedral can host a procession on this scale, its Gothic proportions being those of nature.

I was not prepared to be as moved as I was that day by the presence of the creatures in the cathedral. I know that the tears that welled up in my eyes when I saw them entering the west-facing doors were shared by thousands of others at that moment. But what impressed me most that morning was that the Church was not telling the people what to believe. They already knew what they believed. That was why they were there. The Church's role was to serve that deep knowing and to help translate it into how we live together with the earth.

Too often in the past our approach to truth has been to assume that we have it and others do not. Consequently, we have thought that our role is to tell people what to believe. We are being invited instead into a new humility, to serve the holy wisdom that is already stirring in the hearts of people everywhere, the growing awareness of earth's interrelatedness and sacredness. An essential feature of rebirthing within the Christian household will be to remember that the well of truth is not ours. It is deep within the earth and deep within the heart of humanity. Our role is to be a servant at that well.

Thomas Berry said that we are living in a moment of grace.[24] By that he meant that we are living in the midst of an awareness of earth's oneness, the likes of which humanity has never known before. We are experiencing a way of seeing that is vital to the healing of the earth. The question is whether we will translate this seeing into action, whether we will apply this awareness to the holy work of transformation. But as Berry went on to say, moments of grace are transient.[25] They are passing. In other words, will we meet this moment or will we miss it?

Chapter 2

Reconnecting with Compassion

A primary feature of the rebirthing of God in our lives, individually and collectively, is to come back into relationship with the true heart of one another and all things. Rebirthing involves a reconnecting with compassion.

On the island of Iona there is a meeting of roads. It is called the Crossroads. It is the only crossroads on Iona. There the east-west road intersects the north-south road. On the weekly pilgrimage around the island we pause at this intersection to ask what are the crossroads of our lives and our world today. In our individual lives, or as families and nations, as religious traditions and as a species, what are the critical junctures at which we stand? How do we know which way to turn?

Gathered as pilgrims at the Iona Crossroads, we listen to words from the wisdom literature of the Hebrew Scriptures. We hear that Lady Wisdom stands "at the crossroads" of life (Proverbs 8:2). She is like a young lover who yearns for us, longing to be one with us (Ecclesiasticus 15:2). One of her characteristics is compassion. She loves "all things that exist" (Wisdom 11:24). At every moment in our lives and on every pathway in the world, do we know that we can access the gift of wisdom? It is deeper than our individual consciousness, deeper than our rationality, deeper than our ego. And it leads us into the way of compassion.

A Revolution of the Spirit

Perhaps the greatest prophet of compassion in the world today is Aung San Suu Kyi (b. 1945). Winner of the Nobel Peace Prize in 1991, she is the leader of the nonviolent movement for democracy in Burma. Since 1962, Burma has been governed by one of the most brutally repressive military regimes in the world. Aung San Suu Kyi—often simply referred to by the international media as Suu Kyi, or with affection by the Burmese people as Daw Suu (Lady Suu) and sometimes just Daw (the Lady)—has been described as Burma's Gandhi. Although now free from detention amid hopeful signs of significant political change in Burma, Suu Kyi has spent most of the last twenty-five years under house arrest.

Suu Kyi describes the movement for change that she is leading as a "revolution of the spirit."[1] True power, she says, comes from within.[2] What guides her in this spiritual revolution on a national scale is the way of compassion. The word *compassion* simply means "being with suffering." She has compassion for her people in their suffering, but her commitment to compassion also extends to the leaders of Burma's military dictatorship—to those who have wronged her, her family, and her nation. "If I had really started hating my captors," she says, "I would have defeated myself."[3] Hatred blinds us to the wisdom in our soul.

> Compassion is about making the connection between the heart of my being and the heart of yours, and following that connection.

Many years ago when my wife and I were hiking in the Cairngorm Mountains of Scotland we had just reached one of the highest peaks, Sgoran Dubh, when a thick cloud descended on us. It covered the mountain. The mist was so thick that we could barely see our outstretched hands. Climbing in the Cairngorms can be dangerous. Every year hikers die in such circumstances, slipping off precipitous cliffs. Sgoran Dubh can be particularly treacherous because a few yards from its summit there is a sheer drop of over two thousand feet into the next glen.

We knew where we were and we had a compass and a map. So we took a reading and, one step at a time, followed our readings of the map and compass down the mountain. There were moments when we could barely believe the compass was right. At times our senses were telling us something entirely different. But we knew that we had to place our faith in the compass. In the end we emerged safely from the cloud down the mountainside.

Notice the similarity between the word *compass* and the word *compassion*. They share an etymological root. The earliest use of the word *compass* does not, of course, refer to the modern hiking compass as we know it, the one I had in hand as we descended the mountain. The word is first used to refer to the mathematical compass, that simple two-pronged device that many of us remember using in grade school to measure the distance between two points and to draw arcs and circles. A compass, then, is used to determine the relationship between two points. The related word *compassion* is about honoring the relationship between two people or between one group and another, and remembering those who suffer. It is about making the connection between the heart of my being and the heart of yours, and following that connection—just as we followed the compass in descending the mist-covered mountain—even when we are filled with doubts as to whether we are moving in the right direction.

The Courage to See

Suu Kyi follows a threefold path of compassion that is directly related to her Buddhist inheritance and practice. She describes this compassionate way as "The courage to see. The courage to feel. And the courage to act."[4] To live compassionately, she says, is to courageously see the connection between ourselves and those who suffer. Not only do we see the connection and become aware of it, but we allow ourselves to feel it. Finally, it is not just to see and feel the connection but to act on it, to courageously take responsibility for those who suffer.

Let us explore this threefold path, one aspect at a time. The courage to see compassionately—what does this mean? Suu Kyi says that human life is "infinitely precious."[5] Compassion is about remembering this, allowing ourselves to see it again and again. It is about making the compass connection between ourselves and the other, never forgetting that the other nation, the other community, the other family's child is as precious as ours. The birth of every child, as Suu Kyi says, is like "a new star in our firmament"—the birth of *every* child.[6]

This is not to romanticize the child or to idealize what is deepest in every human being. Suu Kyi recognizes that there is the capacity for good and the capacity for bad in everyone. It is "a matter of which bits you cultivate."[7] That is, it is a matter of growing compassion, cultivating a way of seeing that focuses on the preciousness at the heart of the other. For Suu Kyi the practice of compassionate seeing is related to the practice of daily meditation. She devotes the first hour of every day to meditative discipline. She calls it a way of "learning awareness."[8] In her hour of meditation, she practices attentiveness. That is where she fine-tunes her faculty of consciousness.

We see compassionate awareness in the Christian Gospel accounts of Jesus. He notices. He allows himself to be conscious of the needs of others—their health, happiness, hunger. In St. Matthew's Gospel there is the story of thousands gathering around Jesus in the countryside, to be in his presence, to be taught by him. And who notices that the crowd is hungry? Jesus himself. He makes the connection between his own needs and their needs. He says, "I have compassion for the crowd" (Matthew 15:32).

Suu Kyi says that compassion is about seeing that the rights of others are "as important as defending one's own susceptibilities and rights."[9] This is as essential between individuals as it is between families, communities, and nations. Through compassion we move from ego-centrism to ex-centrism. We find our true center not within the limited confines of our own individuality, family, or nationhood but within the connections between us.

A few years ago, during our first Pilgrimage for Change on Iona, an international event designed especially for young leaders, one of the participants was a young man from the United States named Ben. When he arrived he was anxious about his two little children whom he had left with his wife, Jen, back home in Minnesota. Some years earlier Ben and Jen had moved into one of the most violent districts of Minneapolis. They felt called to be there, to be part of transformation in the area. But that was before their children were born.

Now Esme and Kellan were four and two. There had recently been a shooting locally and a violent break-in to the house across the street. Ben doubted whether they had the spiritual resources to sustain their commitment to the area. But a turning point came for Ben on the Iona pilgrimage. He realized in a new way his compass connection with the other families in the neighborhood. He saw the preciousness of his own children in the eyes of *every* child in the neighborhood. At that moment something of his sacred instinct as a father expanded to include them as well. This is seeing with compassion.

Suu Kyi calls the way of compassionate living the full life.[10] We meet people, she says, who have lived until they are one hundred years old, yet they have never done anything for anyone else. This is not living the full life. "To live the full life one must have the courage to bear the responsibility of the needs of others—one must *want* to bear this responsibility."[11] We have become so accustomed to seeing compassion as a duty,

> Suu Kyi calls the way of compassionate living the full life.

almost as a burden, she says, that we fail to see it essentially as a benediction.[12] Compassion can free us from the prison of the ego, whether our individual ego or that of our family, community, or nation. To *want* to bear responsibility for the needs of others is a blessing. It frees us from our narrow self-interest.

The great challenge is to see our connection with those who seem different from us—the nation that does not share our vision, the people whose lifestyle we cannot understand, the individuals or groups who threaten us. Part of Suu Kyi's stature of spirit is her refusal to demonize those who have wronged her. But this, she says, is because she does not forget her relationship with them. They are soldiers, and her father, too, was a soldier. Not only was he a soldier, he led Burma's struggle for independence from British colonial rule and from Japanese occupation. Although he was assassinated when she was only two years old, she remembers as a child being held by his soldiers. They were like her family. "You are not frightened of people whom you do not hate," she says. "It's that straightforward."[13]

But Suu Kyi teaches that the greatest obstacle to compassion is not hatred. It is habitual patterns of narrow self-interest.[14] It is a way of seeing in which we pretend that we can be well simply by looking after ourselves. Or we pretend that our nation can be safe simply by focusing on the protection of our nation, even at the expense of other nations. Such patterns of narrow self-interest become the norm, accepted and sanctioned at times even by our religious traditions. We become blind to the courage to see.

The Courage to Feel

The second path of Suu Kyi's threefold way of compassion is the courage to feel. It is based on a discourse by the Buddha called the *Metta Sutra*, the compassion teaching. "Like a mother caring for her only child," says the Buddha, so we are to care for one another.[15] As a mother knows the suffering of her own child, so we are to feel the suffering of others.

In the Roofless Church of New Harmony, there is the *Descent of the Spirit* sculpture at one end of the church and at the east end another piece of art. It is by the American sculptor Stephen De Staebler. It is called the Pietà. Inspired by Michelangelo's work of the same name, it is the figure of a mother with her crucified son. But the New Harmony Pietà is of a naked primitive feminine form. In her sides and in her feet are the nail marks of crucifixion. Emerging from her breast is the head of her crucified son.

We know exactly what the sculpture is saying: that when our son suffers, when our daughter has been hurt, when one we love is in agony, we experience that loved one's pain not from afar. We know it as ours. We experience it as if the pain were emerging from our own heart.

My father was a man of great feeling. He might not have described his journey in terms of Suu Kyi's threefold way of compassion, but he saw and felt compassionately, and his actions flowed from his feelings. When I was still a young student, he was involved in international refugee work, enabling thousands of refugees from war-torn Southeast Asia and Africa to find sanctuary in Canada.

My father often needed to be away from home for long periods of time to do his work. This was difficult for him. He loved his family. So, in those days when telecommunications did not so easily allow regular contact from afar, it was his practice when traveling to speak into a cassette tape recorder every day. He would tell us where he was, what he had been doing, whom he had met. Then, every week, he would send a tape home to us.

On one occasion when he had been in a refugee camp for Cambodians in the wake of the Killing Fields, he got into a car at the end of a long day's work to be driven to his accommodation for the night. In the camp

> Suu Kyi teaches that the greatest obstacle to compassion is not hatred. It is habitual patterns of narrow self-interest.

that day he had been meeting parents who had lost their children and children who had lost their parents. He wanted to tell us about them. So in the car he began to record. But when he tried to speak he started to weep. The extraordinary thing about that moment is that he chose not to stop the tape or to erase it. So what I heard as a young man when I listened to the recording was the sound of my father weeping for a few minutes.

How can we choose not to turn off the tape? How can we remain open to the flow of feeling that is an essential part of the pathway of compassion? I believe that if my father had shut down to tears in his life, he would not have been able to do what he did. There is a direct relationship between allowing ourselves to truly feel and the decision to act. Compassionate action is sustained by the courage to feel.

The Greek origin of the word used in our Christian Scriptures to describe compassionate response to the suffering of others does not simply suggest seeing with compassion. It is not even just about feeling with compassion. It is about the very innards of our being flowing with compassion. It is about being moved in our guts. This is how Jesus is described in the Gospel of St. Luke when he sees a mother who has lost her only son. She is a widow and is now following the body of her son for burial in the funeral procession. When Jesus sees her, he has "compassion for her" (Luke 7:13). The Greek verb used is *splagchnizomai,* the same word that is translated elsewhere as "bowels of compassion" (1 John 3:17, KJV).

I felt something like this in my father's tears that day as I listened to his weeping. It came from a deep place within him—the deep place we are being invited to reconnect to within ourselves. Compassion is at the heart of our being, waiting to flow again for one another and for those who suffer. Part of the rebirthing of God in our lives and our world is allowing these depths to flow.

In the last months of my father's life, as dementia was rapaciously taking his memory and mind from us, I witnessed the river of feeling flowing strong in him. In fact, it was flowing more uninhibitedly than ever before. Throughout my father's life, one of his favorite blessings was the prayer attributed to Aaron in the Hebrew Scriptures, sometimes called the Priestly Blessing. It begins with the words, "The Lord bless you and keep you. The Lord make his face to shine upon you" (Numbers 6:24–25). In my father's flow of feeling now, he wanted to give this blessing to everyone, everywhere, repeatedly.

During my last visit to Canada before he entered a nursing home, my sister asked if I would help sell the family car, which my father was still trying to drive, illegally. I called the local car salesman and set up an appointment for the next day. I made a point of saying to him, "When you meet my father tomorrow you will notice that he seems confused about all sorts of things. But please honor him by speaking to him, not me. This is his car. And I'll be there with him."

The young salesman totally got the point. There was playful banter and repartee. My father never lost his sense of humor. There were, of course, absurd moments in the conversation, as there always are when you are dealing with dementia. My father tried to say to him, "Now how much money do I owe you for this car?" The salesman replied, "No, no, Dr. Newell. We want to give you money for the car." To which my father said, looking at me, "This is very generous of them!"

At the end of the transaction, as the check was being handed over to my father, I said to the young salesman, "Whenever I part from my father or whenever we finish a telephone conversation, he gives me a blessing. And I think he would like to bless you now." So there we were, standing in the middle of a car showroom. My father took the salesman's hand, looked straight into his eyes, and said, "The Lord bless you and keep you. The Lord make his face to shine upon you and be gracious to you. The Lord lift up his countenance upon you and give you peace."

I stood gazing at my father, thinking, if only I could be such a bearer of blessing in the world. And then I looked at the young car salesman. Tears were streaming down his face. He will never forget that moment. Never. Do we know that we carry within us for one another the blessing of God? Do we know that the springs of compassion deep within us can flow again?

The Courage to Act

The third pathway of Suu Kyi's commitment to compassion is the courage to act. "Love is an action," she says, "not just a mind state."[16] Buddhism is known for its beautiful practice of sending thoughts of loving-kindness. This is a significant aspect of Buddhist training. But it is not enough to just feel for those who are suffering. We must show compassion, translate it into action. This, says Suu Kyi, is "engaged Buddhism ... active compassion."[17]

One of the most well-known stories in our Christian tradition is Jesus's parable of the Good Samaritan. The Good Samaritan not only sees that an innocent traveler has been robbed and beaten up, he feels for him and acts. "He went to him and bandaged his wounds," said Jesus, "having poured oil and wine on them. Then he put him on his own animal, brought him to an inn, and took care of him" (Luke 10:34).

There were two others on that same road who saw the man who had been robbed, but they "passed by on the other side." First there was a priest. Then there was a respectable leader of the people. They saw the wronged traveler. They may have even felt sorry for him. The problem was they did not act.

The challenge when it comes to compassionate action is that it is costly. Is that not why we so often shut down feelings of compassion and, even before that, refuse to see with compassion? One flows naturally into the other. If we allow ourselves to see, we will more readily feel, and if we open to the river of compassionate feeling, we will more likely act. But the call to action is usually the sticking point.

Gerard W. Hughes, the Scottish Jesuit priest and author of *God of Surprises,* likes to tell the imaginary story of Jesus visiting a modern family. The family is absolutely thrilled to have Jesus in their home. They are so thrilled that they decide to throw a party to introduce him to their friends. They love showing off Jesus. The party is a great success. The problem comes, however, when Jesus decides to stay. In fact, he decides to move in!

This is very different from throwing a party. Jesus begins to bring all sorts of questionable types from the city streets back to the house. A lot of food is being consumed. The neighbors are complaining about plunging property values. It is all becoming far too demanding for the family. But then one of them has a bright idea. When Jesus is having his afternoon siesta, they will brick up his bedroom door. Then they will place a little altar in front of it, with beautiful candlesticks and a silver crucifix, and every time they pass the bedroom they will genuflect. This is how to deal with Jesus!

Sometimes the problem with action is that we become overwhelmed by the complexity of what needs to be done. We feel ill equipped to address the scale and the intricacies of the sheer amount of suffering that we witness around us and in our world. For Suu Kyi it is a matter of returning again and again to what she calls the "profound simplicity" of compassion.[18]

The two most important influences in her life were her father and the teachings of Mahatma Gandhi. In some ways, of course, these two men were significantly different. One was the founder of the modern Burmese army and led a military revolt against the Japanese occupation of Burma. The other believed that only nonviolence was to be used to free his people from the British domination of India. What characterized them both, however, was a profound simplicity of conviction—compassion for the most powerless of their people. It meant that they determined the rightness of any action on the basis of what impact that action would have on the poorest of their brothers and sisters. For both these men, profound simplicity of compassion was the touchstone of their greatness.

A number of years ago I had a dream in which I was running for president of the United States. In the dream Barack Obama was also running. But there was no ego competition between us. Both of us were simply offering ourselves for a job that had to be done. Obama was even giving me advice about how to handle an upcoming live national television interview. And Michelle, too, was trying to be helpful. She told me that I should arrive on time for the broadcast!

In the dream I was feeling overwhelmed. What on earth was I going to say in the interview about my economic and environmental policies? How would I approach the details of international relations and conflict? Before the broadcast I was shown to a changing room, where I sat alone. There I had my realization. I knew what my essential stance would be on every issue. Yes, of course, I would require all sorts of detailed assistance from experts in the various fields, but I knew what would guide me in every decision. I had not yet heard the phrase *profound simplicity,* yet in the dream I realized I would decide every issue from the standpoint of how it would affect all of us. On the environment I would ask not what is best for us alone—for our class, nation, species—but what is best for the whole and for the relationship between all things—for every class, nation, and species. The same would apply on every issue. The heart of the matter was profoundly straightforward. As the dream came to an end, I was still in the changing room but I decided there was no need to outwardly change at all. I would just wear my blue jeans for the broadcast and that would be fine. What the dream did not show me, however, is whether or not I won!

The dream was all about profound simplicity. It focused on not getting so caught up in the complexity of detail that the essence—the compass connection between us—becomes blurred. It reminded me of the importance of the place of transformation in our lives—the changing room—the places and disciplines of solitude in which to access the wisdom that is within us.

Part of what can prevent us from carrying out compassionate action is not only the complexity of what needs to be done in our lives and our world, but the sheer amount of mess and even chaos within us and between us. Suu Kyi uses the analogy of a pressure cooker exploding in the kitchen. There is soup everywhere, all over the ceiling and walls. At such moments we may feel paralyzed. Where do we begin? How can this possibly be cleaned up? Suu Kyi's advice is to just start somewhere. "Don't just stand there despairing," she says. "Do something."[19]

If we just start somewhere in our work of compassionate action, before we know it we find that we are beginning to make some inroads into tidying up the mess. Just start somewhere. We may not know exactly how our action is going to play out. "Just continue to do what you believe is right," says Suu Kyi. "Later on the fruits of what you do will become apparent on their own."[20]

Such an action on April 5, 1989, ended up multiplying the fruits of nonviolent action for change across Burma. Suu Kyi was planning to speak that day at a public forum in the Irrawaddy District, south of Rangoon. This contravened the military junta's law that gatherings of more than four individuals were illegal. As she walked down the road toward the meeting place with some of her supporters, six soldiers at the head of the street leveled their rifles at her and an Army captain ordered her to stop. Sensing there might be trouble, Suu Kyi decided that the right thing to do at that moment, in order to minimize bloodshed, was to instruct her companions to wait at the side of the road while she herself continued walking toward the soldiers. The captain was giving the final countdown to shoot when, at the last second, an Army major standing nearby countermanded the order. Suu Kyi was allowed to pass. Reports of her courageous action spread like wildfire throughout Burma. She exemplified the courage to act—a single act that multiplied actions of courage across the whole nation.

Suu Kyi observes that "those who are doing nothing to improve the world have no hope for it."[21] There is a direct relationship between hope and action. Yes, hope will lead us to act in the first place. But then action, in turn, strengthens hope. When we act with compassion, even if we perform the simplest of compassionate deeds, we recognize that the unjust wrongs that create suffering in our world are not an indelible feature of reality. They can be changed. Suu Kyi is fond of quoting Václav Havel, the leader of the nonviolent revolution in Czechoslovakia in 1989. Commenting on the beginnings of his own commitment to action, he said, "I stopped waiting for the world to improve and exercised my right to intervene in that world."[22]

Suu Kyi never gives up hope, and part of that hope is exercising her responsibility to act for change. When asked by an interviewer about the irredeemable nature of the military dictatorship in Burma, she answered by saying, "How do you know they are irredeemable?"[23] It is not for us to decide who is redeemable and who is not. To say that we have not yet been able to redeem particular wrongs and injustices is not to say that others will not be able to. Our responsibility is to do what we can—the courage to see, the courage to feel, the courage to act.

> Part of what can prevent us from carrying out compassionate action is not only the complexity of what needs to be done in our lives and our world, but the sheer amount of mess and even chaos within us and between us.

The role of true prophets is to point beyond themselves to the work that we are all destined to be part of. Suu Kyi is clear about this in her leadership of Burma's spiritual revolution. She models the rebirth that we are all called to. Whenever interviewers try to inflate her significance, or focus solely on her work for change, Suu Kyi's response is to emphasize that no single one of us is all-important. But each one of us, she says, is essential.[24] Do we believe this? We may not all be called onto the world stage of political action. But each one of us has a critical role to play in our families, our personal relationships, our religious communities. No one else can play that role of compassion for us. Do we know this, that each one of us is essential?

Chapter 3

Reconnecting with the Light

John the Beloved, in the prologue to his Gospel, speaks of "the Light that enlightens every person coming into the world" (John 1:9, adapted). One of the features of the rebirthing of God is reconnecting with this Light. It is the Light at the heart of every newborn child. It is the Light at the heart of all life.

Turn But a Stone and an Angel Moves

On the isle of Iona, one of the places we stop in our weekly pilgrimage is the Hill of the Angels on the Atlantic side of the island. It sits on the edge of the Machair, which in Gaelic simply means "raised beach." Thousands of years of sea spray crashing onto the bay at the back of the ocean has produced the sandy soil of the Machair, now used by the island farmers—or crofters, as they are called—as a place of common grazing. It is also the island golf course, a full eighteen holes! The sheep and cattle keep it trimmed.

The Machair is a place of extraordinary light, sitting as it does on the edge of the Atlantic Ocean. The combination of clear air, coming in off thousands of miles of expansive sea, plus the light, especially at sunset, produces a glory of brilliance. The landscape glistens. As George MacLeod, founder of the modern-day Iona community, writes in one of his prayers, "The grass is vibrant, the rocks pulsate, ... turn but a stone and an angel moves."[1] In May there is a carpet of crimson-tipped daisies and shining yellow buttercups. It is a dreamland of light. In June the Machair is edged by wild yellow irises and in August by the purple of blooming heather.

It is said that in the sixth century this is where St. Columba would come to pray each day at sunset. He would perch at the top of the hillock beside the Machair and gaze out to the west as the sun dipped into the ocean. The Pulitzer Prize–winning poet Mary Oliver (b. 1935) writes of such a moment:

> Have you ever seen
> anything
> in your life
> more wonderful
>
> than the way the sun,
> every evening,
> relaxed and easy,
> floats towards the horizon
>
> and in the clouds or the hills,
> or the rumpled sea,
> and is gone—
> and how it slides again
>
> out of the blackness,
> every morning,
> on the other side of the world,
> like a red flower
>
> streaming upward on its heavenly oils,
> say, on a morning in early summer,
> at its perfect imperial distance—
> and have you ever felt for anything

such wild love—
do you think there is anywhere, in any language,
a word billowing enough
for the pleasure

that fills you,
as the sun
reaches out,
as it warms you

as you stand there,
empty-handed—
or have you too
turned from this world—

or have you too
gone crazy
for power,
for things?[2]

Legend has it that Columba chose to pray alone at the setting of the sun. It was his time of solitude, so he would tell his community not to follow him to the Machair. There was one young monk, however, who could not resist witnessing what the great man did when he prayed alone. The monk followed Columba late in the day by sneaking through the next valley, the Glen of the Fairies. There he hid behind a rock at the top of a promontory from which he was able to see Columba praying. What he saw were angels of light ascending and descending all around the saint. So the hillock on which Columba prayed each evening came to be known as the Hill of the Angels.

Columba's story echoes that of Jacob in the Hebrew Scriptures, who dreams of a ladder that connects heaven and earth. Moving up and down that ladder are angels of light. Jacob had been sent into exile by his mother, Rebekah, who feared that her twin sons, Jacob and Esau, would kill each other in their quarreling. Just as Jacob was heading into the strange territory of a new land, filled with uncertainty, he was visited in his sleep by an angel, and he dreamed of messengers of light ascending and descending all around him. When he awakened from sleep, he said, "Surely the Lord is in this place—and I did not know it.... This is none other than the house of God, and this is the gate of heaven" (Genesis 28:16–17).

In the Celtic world that gateway is present everywhere. In every place is the immediacy of heaven. In every moment we can glimpse the Light that was in the beginning and from which all things have come. As Oliver says, "The threshold is always near."[3] We can step over this threshold and back again in the fleeting span of a second. In a single step we can find ourselves momentarily in that other world, the world of eternal Light, which is woven inseparably through this world—the world of matter that is forever unfolding like a river in flow.

George MacLeod spoke of Iona as a thin place. It is a place in which we sometimes see briefly through the veil that separates heaven and earth. At times that veil can seem as "thin as gossamer."[4] But to say that Iona is a thin place is not to say that every other place is thick. Rather, it is to say that Iona, and similar sacred sites of pilgrimage and healing throughout the world, are like sacraments or living icons through which we glimpse the Light that is present everywhere. Iona is not a place to cling to, or escape to, but to cherish as a place in which our seeing is renewed, so that when we return to the demanding and conflicted places of our lives and our world we do so with open eyes that have been refreshed.

The Light at the Center of Every Cell

Mary Oliver is one of the great prophets of Light in our modern world. She speaks of "the light at the center of every cell."[5] It is not just a feature of life that may or may not be present in different people, places, and creatures. It is the essence of life, the center from which all things have their being. The Celtic world celebrates this as the Light within all life. New science views it as the light that burst the universe into being at the beginning of time, and that still pulsates at the heart of everything that has been created. Oliver invites us to be aware of this Light and to live in open-eyed wonder of it, "to be dazzled," as she says, and to see that "The light is everything."[6]

Oliver's sense that the Light is "at the center of every cell," and that it is everything, is similar to the vision of the early Celtic prophet John Scotus Eriugena in the ninth century, who said that the Light of God is the "Essence of all things."[7] He uses the analogy of lines coming out from a single point. The further out any line moves, the more divergent it appears from the other lines. But when we trace any of the lines back to their source, we find the common point from which all the lines have come. So it is, he says, with everything that has being. Everything originates in the Light of God. If somehow that Light were extracted from the universe, all things would cease to exist.

Eriugena loves to play with words. One such word is the Greek noun for God, *theos*. It derives, he says, from the Greek verb *theo*, which means to run or flow.[8] God is the Light that flows through all things. It is like a subterranean river running deep in the folds of the universe. Without it there would be no life. The Scottish poet Kenneth White (b. 1936) builds on Eriugena's playful interpretation when he speaks of this river at the heart of all things as the "glow-flow."[9] What we are called to do, says White, is not just look at the flow, not merely analyze it, but know that we are part of it and dive more deeply into it.

"My work is loving the world," says Oliver, "which is mostly standing still and learning to be astonished."[10] As she writes elsewhere:

> It doesn't have to be
> the blue iris, it could be
> weeds in a vacant lot, or a few
> small stones; just
> pay attention, then patch
>
> a few words together and don't try
> to make them elaborate, this isn't
> a contest but the doorway
>
> into thanks, and a silence in which
> another voice may speak.[11]

What she is describing is a movement from awareness into open-eyed wonder, and from awe to prayer, and from prayer to adoration.

Eriugena teaches that because the Light of God is the "Essence of all things," everything should be regarded as a theophany, a showing or revealing of the Divine. The deeper we move in relation to any created thing, the closer we come to the "divine brilliance" at the heart of life.[12] "It is not hard to understand where God's body is," says Oliver. "It is everywhere and everything."[13]

In 2013 my wife and I spent some time in Pondicherry at the Indian ashram of Sri Aurobindo (1872–1950). Sri Aurobindo was, at one stage in his life, a freedom fighter engaged in secret revolutionary activity to cast off British domination in India. In 1908 he was arrested by the British Raj and imprisoned. During his year of solitary confinement in Alipore, Sri Aurobindo had a spiritual experience that changed his life. He saw that there could be true transformation in the world only by opening to the Light that is in all things.

In 1926 Sri Aurobindo established his ashram in Pondicherry to serve this vision of peaceful transformation between nations and religions. Mirra Alfassa (1878–1973), a young woman of Jewish-French origin, joined him and became his closest spiritual colleague and successor. After Sri Aurobindo's death in 1950, Alfassa conceived the idea of creating a town committed to human unity, based on Sri Aurobindo's belief that the Divine Light is within all people, deeper than any division between nations or religions. In the 1960s, that vision began to become a reality as Alfassa worked to build a town that she named Auroville, just outside Pondicherry. In 1968 the United Nations endorsed it as a city that belongs not to one nation or one religion but to the whole world and to every people. There are now over two thousand people from over fifty nations living in Auroville.

> In the Celtic world [the] gateway is present everywhere. In every place is the immediacy of heaven. In every moment we can glimpse the Light that was in the beginning and from which all things have come.

Inspired by Alfassa, the citizens of Auroville began to build the Matrimandir (Temple of the Mother). This temple celebrates the Womb of Light from which we and all things have come. Its structure is an enormous golden sphere, 120 feet across. It has twelve earthen ramparts that curve up toward it, giving the impression that the dome is rising out of the earth. Sri Aurobindo taught that the Divine Light is within matter. It is to be found not by looking away from the earth but by looking within everything that emerges from the earth.

The inner chamber of the temple is completely white—white marble walls, twelve white massive pillars, and white carpeting throughout. It is a place of silence—no words, no ritual, no religious form or sound. There is an aperture at the top of the sphere through which a single beam of sunlight enters. Above the aperture are prisms that track the sun's light during the day to reflect the beam directly into the chamber. At the heart of the temple is a great crystal-glass globe, thirty inches in diameter, into which the beam of light enters and then refracts to fill the whole temple. This, said Alfassa, is the most important thing about the Matrimandir—the light at its center. It is the Light at the heart of all life.

The Temple of the Mother is not an end in itself. It is a sanctuary of Light that inspires the work of transformation. Since the inception of Auroville in the 1960s the community has planted over eighteen million trees in the surrounding territory and has turned what was desertified land into a garden of abundance. The planted trees have allowed the water table to rise for the entire region. No longer do the torrential rains that fall during the monsoon season simply run off to the sea. The land now holds the rainfall, sustaining an abundance of crops, not only for the citizens of Auroville but for the families living in the surrounding area. There is a connection between tending the Light at the center and the well-being of the whole of life—both our own lives and the life of the earth.

We find this same connection at the heart of the Christian household, looking to the Glory at the center of life in such a way that the whole of life is seen to be suffused with that same Light. This is what the story of the nativity of the Christ Child does. The sacredness of the Christ Child, born of the marriage between heaven and earth, reveals the sacredness of the universe, conceived by the union of spirit and matter.

George MacLeod said "matter matters" because at the heart of the physical is the spiritual. Hidden within the mundane is the Divine. What we do to matter, therefore—whether that be the matter of another's body in relationship, or the matter of the earth's body and how we handle its sacred resources, or the matter of the body politic and how we honor the holy sovereignty of one another's nationhood—all of this relates to the Light that we worship in the Christ Child.

Last year I was in Cuba at the beginning of Advent, staying at the Convent of Santa Brigida in Havana. One of the Brigidine sisters had spent days preparing the nativity scene in what historically had been the stable on the ground floor of the convent. Its double doors swing open onto a busy street in Havana. There, hundreds of Cuban families stop every day during the Christmas season to gaze at this life-size representation of the Light of the Christ Child. They gaze with delight not because the nativity scene is pointing them to a foreign figure in a far-off land and age. They gaze because they have recognized something of this Light in the newborn countenance of their own children. And they gaze, I believe, because they are distantly remembering deep within themselves the Light that no darkness on earth can extinguish.

> The deeper we move in relation to any created thing, the closer we come to the "divine brilliance" at the heart of life.

Sister Maria is excited to show me the manger scene and to tell me all about the creativity that goes into preparing it each year; she exudes enthusiasm as she speaks about how Cuban families come from all over the city to stop and stare at this depiction of the Christ Child. But this ties in with the passion she brings to her work year-round among the poorest of Havana. This passion is inextricably linked to the vision of Light that inspires her community to feed the hungry and to welcome strangers as if they were feeding and welcoming Christ. It is no coincidence that, in the thirteenth century, St. Francis first introduced the tradition of the nativity scene. It brought into focus for him the Light that he saw in the earth and in every creature, the light of "Brother Sun" and "Sister Moon," as he called them in his *Canticle of the Sun*, or "Sister Water" and "Brother Fire."

Be Filled with Light and Shine

What are the places that enable us to bring into focus the Light at the heart of life? For Oliver it is when she is in the woods:

> When I am among the trees,
> especially the willows and the honey locust,
> equally the beech, the oaks and the pines,
> they give off such hints of gladness.
> I would almost say that they save me, and daily.
>
> I am so distant from the hope of myself,
> in which I have goodness, and discernment,
> and never hurry through the world
> but walk slowly, and bow often.
>
> Around me the trees stir in their leaves
> and call out, "Stay awhile."
> The light flows from their branches.
>
> And they call again, "It's simple," they say,
> "and you too have come
> into the world to do this, to go easy, to be filled
> with light, and to shine."[14]

Behind our family home in Edinburgh are the Royal Botanic Gardens. Within the gardens is a grove of giant redwoods, named after John Muir (1838–1914), the great nineteenth-century American environmentalist. In Scotland, however, we claim him as ours. He was born in Dunbar, down the coast from Edinburgh. Every day I go to the John Muir Grove to remember the Light. I stand in the midst of the redwoods, or lean against one of their mighty trunks, gazing up through their heights into the infinity of heaven. There I remember the One-ness of which I am a part, the Light that streams through me, you, and all things.

Muir called these great trees, and the Californian mountains in which they naturally grow, "God's first temples."[15] In such temples—and in the sanctuaries of silence that we seek out in our city gardens or in our individual homes, sitting attentively by an open window looking to the east as the sun rises with its first light—we remember why we have come into the world, "to be filled with light, and to shine."

For Oliver this means looking upon everything as "a brother-hood and a sisterhood"[16] and remembering our place in the "family of things."[17] It means knowing that we have a sibling relationship with everything that exists and that the Light that we glimpse in the trees, in the creatures, in the eyes of another, is the Light that is also within us. Do we know that we are bearers of this unspeakably beautiful Light? Do we know that this Light at the heart of our being is for one another and for the world?

To be bearers of Light—which is pure gift and not of our own doing—means that we are made to shine. But when we truly shine, and when we work for the true shining of every child, woman, man, and creature, we find that sometimes we create discomfort in the people around us and in the holders of power in our communities and our world. Not only do they feel uncomfortable; sometimes they feel threatened. This is as true in our personal relationships and workplaces as it is in the great struggles of communities and nations. Those who cling to power for their own sake, or for the sake only of their chosen communities and their special interest groups, do not want everyone to shine. The shadow side of power is a determination that only some should shine, and that only some should be considered worthy.

This is why Jesus was crucified by the Roman governor of Palestine and why Archbishop Oscar Romero (1917–1980) of El Salvador was assassinated by a death squad of his country's military junta. Identifica-tion with the poor is a threat to those in power. For the same reason, Mahatma Gandhi, as we shall see later, was murdered by one of his own, an Indian Hindu, for teaching that Muslims as well as Hindus shine and were to be regarded by Hindus as brothers and sisters. Over the centuries, countless women have been branded and burned as "witches" because the Light of their feminine wisdom threatened a system that was dominated by male power. To shine, we need to keep returning to the places—whether our magnificent religious sanctuaries of Light or earth's natural temples of Light—to remember that we and all things have come into the world to be filled with this Light and to shine.

The angel of Light who blessed Jacob at the beginning of his exile, and showed him in a dream the ladder that connects heaven and earth, was the same angel who led him back to Esau after long years of separation. On the night before he met his estranged brother, Jacob struggled with fear. How would Esau greet him? Would it be with disapproval, with anger, with violence? So Jacob wrestled through the night with the angel who was guiding him. It is even said that Jacob was wounded in this struggle and for the rest of his life walked with a limp. But in the morning light, says Genesis, when the brothers approached one another from afar, "Esau ran to meet him, and embraced him, and fell on his neck and kissed him, and they wept" (Genesis 33:4).

> Hidden within the mundane is the Divine. What we do to matter, therefore, all of this relates to the Light that we worship in the Christ Child.

There is a relationship between Light and reconciliation. There is an essential link between growing in an awareness of the Light that has been showered upon all things and the work of coming back into relationship with all things. "To see your face," said Jacob to Esau, "is like seeing the face of God" (Genesis 33:10). To be truly reconciled *is* to see the Light at the heart of the other.

But we need more than just reconciliation with one another as human beings and nations. We also need reconciliation with all species of the earth. They are our brothers and sisters, says Oliver. "They are the family we have run away from."[18] At birth we knew this. As children we were naturally aware of—sometimes even spellbound by—the

Light that is in all things. But then it was educated out of us. And we began to forget.

The English poet William Blake (1757–1827) tells the story from boyhood of seeing a tree filled with angels of light. He runs home with great excitement to tell his father what he has seen, but his father responds by saying that if he ever tells him a "lie" like this again he will beat him.[19] Our materialistic culture and, at times, our religion in its dualistic separation of spirit and matter, have been part of beating this out of us. In the power structures of our communities and nations, we need to ask who is being served by such perspectives? We need to decide that no longer will we deny the Light that is in our sibling species and in the matter of earth's resources. It is the Glory at the heart of me, you, and all things.

Letting Go to the Light

Oliver as a prophet calls us to see this Light and to consciously carry it in our lives for one another. But she also warns us not to confuse this Light with our egos or to cling to its glorious manifestations, including the earth in its grandeur, our religious traditions and their great sanctuaries of wonder, or ourselves and the beauty we see in another's eyes. As Oliver writes:

> To live in this world
>
> you must be able
> to do three things:
> to love what is mortal;
> to hold it
>
> against your bones knowing
> your own life depends on it;
> and, when the time comes to let it go,
> to let it go.[20]

We are never to forget that the Light is untameable and unnameable. We are to remember that we are messengers of a Light that precedes us—from which we and all things have come—as well as a Light that will continue to flow long after us, infinitely unfolding into forms that we know nothing of yet. As Oliver asks, "What does the world mean to you if you can't trust it to go on shining when you're not there?"[21]

Iona is a thin place. It is a place where we more readily remember that the "threshold is always near," that we can fleetingly step over that threshold, over and back, over and back into the world of Light from which all worlds have come. A number of years ago, one of our Iona pilgrimages included a couple named Larry and Bunny from Texas. They had been married for over half a century and clearly they were still in love. During dinner together on the first evening of the pilgrimage, a conversation arose about death. The question that was posed was this: If you could choose, how would you like to die? Bunny was the first to respond. "I would like to die in my sleep," she said. We went to bed that night and Bunny died in her sleep.

> When we truly shine, and when we work for the true shining of every child, woman, man, and creature, we find that sometimes we create discomfort in the people around us and in the holders of power in our communities and our world.

When I saw Larry the next morning, he was sobbing with grief. His whole being was shaking with the shock of loss. But amid his tears he said to me that I should continue my teaching with the group that day. He also said that he wanted to remain with us on pilgrimage for the rest of the week. That, he said, would be Bunny's desire. This ran contrary to all my pastoral instincts. I thought he should immediately return home to be with his family in Texas. But later that day he spoke with his children and grandchildren. And they agreed with Larry. "Stay on pilgrimage," they said, "and when you return home we will do our grieving together."

Larry showed us his brokenness that week. He vulnerably and beautifully opened his grieving to us, making this a most memorable pilgrimage. We experienced the thinness of this world. It was as if

Bunny were there leading us over and back, over and back, across the threshold between the seen and the unseen. We were being led through the veil that is as "thin as gossamer" to glimpse the Light from which we and all things have come.

That Light is here and now. The gateway is all around us and within us. As the Qur'an says, whichever way you look, "There is the face of God" (Cow 2:115). It is a Light that is forever waiting to come forth again in new ways. To reconnect to that Light—in our individual lives, families, communities, and religious traditions—will again be to bear blessing for the world.

We are invited to pay attention, to see the Light that is at the heart of this moment and every moment, to know that we are full of Light and can shine, and when the time comes to let it go, to let go of even our most cherished embodiments of Light. But, above all else, says Oliver, we are to love the Light and keep giving ourselves to it:

> When it's over, I want to say: all my life
> I was a bride married to amazement.
> I was the bridegroom, taking the world into my arms.
>
> .....
>
> I don't want to end up simply having visited this world.[22]

Chapter 4

Reconnecting with the Journey

W e are made "in the image of God" (Genesis 1:27) or, as Julian of Norwich puts it, we are made "of God."[1] Similarly the prologue to St. John's Gospel speaks of "the Light that enlightens every person coming into the world" (John 1:9, adapted). These teachings invite us to remember what we so frequently forget, that what is deepest in us is sacred.

Where do we look, therefore, for wisdom? Where is truth to be found? Not away from our depths, but deep within the mystery of our being, every human being, and every great wisdom tradition. As much as the species of the earth need one another to be well, so we need one another as religious traditions. Our true well-being will be found in relationship, not in isolation.

One of the primary features of the rebirthing of God is reconnecting with wisdom, allowing the truth that has been etched into our being to come forth in new ways. This reconnection will happen through a journey into the forgotten and unknown depths of our own souls and traditions. It will also include an outward journey into the neglected lands and undiscovered territories of other ways of seeing and other religious inheritances. The historic religions of the world are given not to compete with each other but to complete each other.

Journeying into Unknown Territory

Perhaps the most cherished station on the Iona pilgrimage is St. Columba's Bay at the south end of the island. Legend has it that Columba landed here on Pentecost Day in 563 CE. It is a bay of ocean-smoothed rounded stones that the wild sea has been casting onto this shore for thousands of years. Here Columba and his disciples landed in their journey from Ireland into the unknown territory of Scotland. Although its official name is St. Columba's Bay, its name in the hearts of many of us who have experienced this place, and perhaps also in Columba's heart, is the Bay of New Beginnings. For it was here that Columba experienced a new beginning in his life.

There are various legends as to why Columba came to Iona. He was an Irish prince of royal blood. But he was also a monk and a leader in his monastic community. Some say that he was forced to flee Ireland because of his refusal to bend his knee to imperial Christianity's attempt to impose uniformity. The Mediterranean mission that had become dominant in Ireland was insisting on a clerical tonsure that had its origin in Rome, the priestly practice of shaving the top of one's head of hair as a sign of devotion to Christ. The Celtic mission, on the other hand, wore the Irish tonsure, the head shaved at the back and sides. The origin of this was the Druidic tonsure that had been used in the ancient Celtic world by the holy teachers of pre-Christian wisdom. Columba chose the path of continuity with the truths that preceded Christianity in Ireland. He spoke of Christ as his "Druid."[2] This was his way of radically affirming the relationship between Christianity and the ancient nature-based wisdom traditions that preceded it in Ireland and throughout the Celtic world.

Another strand of legend suggests that Columba came to Iona in penitential exile from his homeland. He had sparked a feud among monastic communities by copying, without permission, the sacred manuscript of another monastery. Blood was shed in the feud and Columba, taking responsibility for the battle, accepted exile as penance for his wrongdoing. So he set sail, with twelve of his monastic community, to a land from which Ireland could not be seen.

Whatever the reason for Columba's journey to Iona, he was moving from home into the strange territory of a new land, from what was known and familiar to what was alien and unknown. St. Columba's Bay was a bay of new beginnings in Columba's life. It was also a bay of new beginnings in the life of a whole nation. Here Scottish Christianity was born. Over the centuries, the waters of this bay have been the waters of new birth for thousands of pilgrims seeking new beginnings in their lives and their world.

The practice of peregrination was strong in the Celtic world. It often involved setting sail from one's homeland as a pilgrim, from what was known and comfortable into what was unknown and challenging. Peregrination was sometimes described as "seeking the place of one's resurrection," leaving the familiar in order to experience new birth, dying to the boundaries and securities of home to be alive to what one had never imagined before.[3]

The Abrahamic faiths of Judaism, Christianity, and Islam are characterized by the practice of pilgrimage. There are principal destinations, like Jerusalem, Mount Sinai, and Mecca. And there are many other cherished routes, like the path to Santiago de Compostella in Spain, or the journey to Iona in the Western isles of Scotland, and the many sites associated with beloved teachers like Rumi, Francis, and Julian. This is true of all the great religions of the world. But in the Abrahamic family, the motif of journeying toward new beginnings can be found as early as the book of Genesis. "Go to the land that I will show you ... [and there] I will bless you ... and in you all the families of the earth shall be blessed" (Genesis 12:1–3).

Theologian Thomas Berry speaks of the microphase and the macrophase of any religious tradition.[4] During its microphase, when it is still very young and its particular gifts for the world are just forming, the tradition needs to protect its uniqueness by well-defined boundaries.

> One of the primary features of the rebirthing of God is reconnecting with wisdom, allowing the truth that has been etched into our being to come forth in new ways.

It is like a newly planted sapling that requires protection in order to grow. During that microphase the blessings of the tradition are primarily for those who come within its self-defined boundaries. Those who "belong" to the tradition benefit from its particular graces and ministrations. During a religion's macrophase, however, when it has grown up, when it is well established, a religious tradition can offer its blessings freely to the world.

It is time for Christianity to enter its macrophase. It is time for us to grow into the maturity of our Christhood and make our offerings freely to the world. Not on the basis of whether people become Christian and choose to enter our household, but on the basis of the gifts that we have to offer for the well-being of the world. Think of the way in which Hinduism in its maturity has blessed humanity with a single word, *Namaste*. This ancient Sanskrit greeting has become common parlance throughout the world. It means "The Divine in me honors the Divine in you," "The Sacred in me bows to the Sacred in you." Hinduism has freely given this away to the world. There are no strings attached, no accompanying conditions. We do not have to become Hindu to use the phrase.

What is it that a grown-up Christianity has to freely offer the world? There is so much treasure in our household that we could generously distribute. We hold within our Scriptures an awareness of earth's sacredness that could more deeply serve today's environmental movements. We have inherited from Jesus a vision of nonviolence that could profoundly redirect our nations from conflict to peace. We have been taught practices of compassion for those who are poor and hungry and sick that could play a foundational role in the well-being of any society. There is no shortage of treasure in our household. What do we need to give away freely to the world and what do we need to receive from humanity's other great religious traditions?

Traveling as Pilgrims

One of our great modern Christian prophets of journeying into the unknown territory of another tradition in order to give and receive was Father Bede Griffiths (1906–1993). He was an English Benedictine monk who spent most of his life in India. There, he said, he found the other half of his soul.[5] Even as a young man entering the strange territory of Hinduism and India for the first time, he spoke of journeying as a pilgrim.[6] To him, being a pilgrim meant approaching the East not only to offer his Christian treasure but also to deeply receive the gifts of Hinduism. Think of how different our Christian history might have been if we had journeyed as pilgrims toward the people and religious traditions of other nations.

Many years ago I was delivering a talk in Ottawa, Ontario, on some of the main themes of the prologue to St. John's Gospel, and especially the words "the Light that enlightens every person coming into the world" (John 1:9, adapted). In attendance that evening was a Canadian Mohawk elder. He had been invited to be there to make observations about the parallels between his First Nations spirituality and the spirituality of the Celtic world. At the end of my talk he stood with tears in his eyes and said, "As I have been listening to these themes, I have been wondering where I would be tonight. I have been wondering where my people would be tonight. And I have been wondering where we would be as a Western world tonight if the mission that had come to us from Europe centuries ago had come expecting to find light in us."

> It is time for Christianity to make our offerings freely to the world. Not on the basis of whether people become Christian and choose to enter our household, but on the basis of the gifts that we have to offer for the well-being of the world.

We cannot undo the tragic wrongs that have been done in the name of Christianity to the First Nations people of Canada and to the indigenous peoples of many nations throughout the world. We cannot undo the unspeakable acts of cruelty and arrogance, perhaps unparalleled in the history of world religion, annihilating and conquering in the name of the truly humble one, Jesus. We can, however, be part of a new beginning. We can allow the true essence of our Christian heritage to be born anew.

Even before Bede Griffiths set sail for India, he was aware of what he called the fossilization of Western Christianity.[7] It had become hardened, stuck both doctrinally and ritually. It was not living and unfolding like the universe, forever seeking new expression and embodiment through relationship. It had become isolated from the other great religious traditions of the world and ossified in its dogmas, paralyzed in the trappings of infallibility. One of the laws of the universe is that if something is not unfolding, it is dying. If it is not sprouting in new directions, it is decaying. Bede was aware of the rot that had developed in his religious tradition. But one of his mantras of belief was that there were "seeds of life in the rotten apple."[8] We need to pay attention to those seeds if there is to be new birth.

By the early 1960s, Bede was leading the Benedictine community of Shantivanam in Tamil Nadu in the southeast of India. There he was giving himself to what he called "the marriage of East and West," allowing the seed-force of Christianity to enter the fertile womb of India's imagination and Hindu wisdom.[9] At morning prayer Christian and Vedic scriptures were read hand in hand. At daily mass, after receiving the bread and wine of the Christian sacrament, worshippers would receive on their foreheads the *bindi*, the red dot of Hinduism that signifies the third eye, or the inner eye of wisdom. To be united with Christ was to be reunited with the wisdom that is deep within us.

> We cannot undo the tragic wrongs that have been done in the name of Christianity … We can, however, be part of a new beginning. We can allow the true essence of our Christian inheritance to be born anew.

This was not syncretism. It was a belief in marriage, in bringing together what had developed separately but could be richer in relationship. It was a belief that true union differentiates, that a commingling in love leads not to uniformity and loss of identity but to the radical freedom of uniqueness and individuality that only love can produce. We know this in our most important relationships. Who are the people who have truly loved us? These are the ones who, in entering union with us, have most set us free to be truly ourselves. So it is, believed Bede, in the most important relationships of our world as nations and religious traditions. True unity, bringing our heart into union with the heart of the other, is the basis of true freedom.

What is it that the East brings to this marriage? What is it that the West carries in its dowry? The West never forgets the transcendence of the Sacred, the otherness of the Divine. Always what cannot be said about God is greater than what can be said. So the West is strong at not confusing us with God, at not forgetting that everything we essentially are is pure grace. The East, on the other hand, never forgets the immanence of the Divine, the within-ness of the Sacred. The deeper we move in any created thing, the closer we come to the One who is the Soul within all souls, the Life within all life. The East focuses on the sacredness of all life.

Bede was not the first Christian to seek the marriage of apparently opposite insights. We find expressions of this in the teachings of Meister Eckhart, the fourteenth-century Christian mystic, who said that God is both "unnameable" and "omninameable."[10] There is nothing that can capture the name or essence of the Divine. So Eckhart knew with the West that the most that can be said about God is that God is not this and not that. The Divine transcends who we are and everything we have ever known or experienced. But God is also omninameable. Everything is essentially an expression, a theophany of the Divine. So Eckhart knew with the East that everything bears the name of God. Everything reflects the Divine. To look into the eyes of another is to look into the depths of the Infinite. Each one of us is an unrepeatable revelation of the One from whom all things have come. The same is true of each creature, each life-form.

The Scottish Jesuit priest Gerard W. Hughes likes to introduce himself at conferences by saying, "Hello. I'm Gerry, a unique manifestation of the Divine." Not a typical Western form of introduction! But think of how we might view ourselves differently, and the true heart of one another and all things, if we tried that out occasionally. I suppose what is more typically Western about Gerry's introduction is the word *unique*. That is part of the gift that we carry in the West, remembering the uniqueness of the individual. The East, on the other hand, knows the oneness of which we are a part. Both West and East, of course, have their shadow sides. On the one hand, an overinflation of individuality comes at the expense of collective consciousness. On the other, an exaggeration of communal identity can diminish attention to our individual rights.

Another aspect of life in which East and West differ is in the approach to the physical reality of the universe. The West tends to view it as permanent, as enduring. The East, on the other hand, sees the physical as impermanent, as passing. The Sanskrit word used to point to the transitoriness of outward reality is *maya*. It has been misinterpreted in the West as "unreality." But by *maya* the East simply means that everything physical is ephemeral. In that sense it has no ultimate reality.

> There is a tendency in the West to absolutize our religion. Instead of viewing it as a road sign that points beyond itself, we consider it a stop sign. It becomes the destination, the end.

The East's sense of the transitory nature of everything physical applies to religion in its outward form as well. It, too, is passing. It points beyond itself to what cannot be named. The West, on the other hand, tends to view religion in absolute terms, especially its central features—the Scriptures, Christ, the doctrine of the Trinity. It does not see these simply as pointing to the eternal but as eternal.

A number of years ago I was preaching at St. Giles Cathedral in Edinburgh. Standing in the pulpit that hugs one of the thousand-year-old central massive pillars, I began the sermon by saying that there would be a time when this building would be no more. There would be a time when our Scriptures would be no more. And there would be a time when Christianity would be no more. At which point a woman in the congregation shouted out, "Heresy!"

This, of course, is when the rest of the congregation woke up. I could see them whispering to each other, "What did he say?" The woman who had shouted was in one of the cathedral's box pews. By now she was standing and had decided to leave in protest. She opened, then slammed shut, the little door at the end of her pew as she headed off, stomping down the central aisle with her hard-heeled shoes, and shouting one more time, "Heresy!"

There is a tendency in the West to absolutize our religion. Instead of viewing it as a road sign that points beyond itself, we consider it a stop sign. It becomes the destination, the end. When that happens, it becomes confused with the Ultimate Reality that is always beyond utterance, beyond embodiment, beyond form. How can we both cherish our religious inheritance—its symbols and sacraments—and at the same time let go of it within ourselves?

Shedding Our Attachment to the Ego

One of the teachers I have worked closely with over the years is Nahum Ward-Lev, a rabbi from Santa Fe, New Mexico. When we first began to teach together, he said of me, "When Philip teaches, it comes out Christian but it goes in Jewish." This has been my experience of him as well. When Nahum teaches Torah, he feeds my devotion to the way of Jesus. How do we do this for each other? We have been taught to see our wisdoms as exclusive of each other so that we fail to see the deeper interwovenness of wisdom between our traditions.

A few summers ago Nahum and I were teaching at Ghost Ranch Conference Center in New Mexico. On this occasion we were teaching separate classes rather than co-teaching, as we have often done. In my group one morning we were reflecting on that beautiful passage in St. John's Gospel in which the risen Christ appears to Mary Magdalene. The scene is the garden in which the body of Jesus had been laid. Mary, intending to visit the tomb, has found that its stone has been rolled away and that the place of burial is empty. She fears that the body of her beloved teacher has been stolen. She is weeping. At this point in the story the risen Christ appears and speaks to her. Mary thinks he is the gardener. But when he calls her by name, she recognizes him. In the dialogue that follows, Jesus says to Mary, "Do not hold on to me.... I am ascending to my Father and your Father, to my God and your God" (John 20:17).

As I reflected on this passage with my group, my mind kept taking me to Nahum. I thought I must speak to him about this story. I was aware that there was one aspect of the reading in particular that was deeply calling my attention: "Do not hold on to me," said Jesus. Already I was beginning to realize that this was the aspect of the story that I especially wanted to share with Nahum. But, at this stage, I was just making an observation, a theological comment about how Christianity had tried to "hold on to" Jesus, how we had tried to make him exclusively ours.

I found Nahum immediately after the class. We ended up together in the same line at lunch so I was able to tell him that I wanted to share something from the morning. We took our trays out to a picnic table that sits under one of the great cottonwood trees. There I began to speak to Nahum about the garden passage in St. John's Gospel. But when I tried to tell the story I began to weep. Instead of a theological observation, it became a confession from my heart and from the heart of Christianity. I needed to ask his forgiveness and the forgiveness of Judaism. We have tried to hold on to Jesus. We have tried to make him exclusively ours, a Christian possession. But he is not ours. He belongs to the world. He was born a Jew, lived as a Jew, and died as a faithful Jew. He is not a Christian, nor was he the founder of our religion. How can we both love him and, at the same time, not clutch him possessively? How can we cherish the gift of his teachings and not claim them solely as ours?

I first visited India in 1990. It was strange territory to me and I had never been part of a deep meeting between religious traditions. Harry Underhill, the nephew of the great English mystic Evelyn Underhill (1875–1941), had invited me to travel with him to India and spend time with Bede Griffiths at his ashram, Shantivanam. Harry felt that the Abbey community on Iona, which my wife and I were the leaders of at that time, could do with some exposure to the East. He was right about that. But maybe even greater than the Abbey's need was my need to learn from the East.

We arrived at night and were shown by Brother Martin to a simple cell that we shared together. Early in the morning, when it was still very dark, a bell rang, announcing morning meditation. Having not yet seen the ashram by daylight, I had to follow the sound of footsteps to the river where dozens of people—monks, villagers, visitors from around the world—were gathered to pray at the rising of the sun. We had been summoned to meditation and there, standing at the water's edge, surrounded by men and women from many nations meditating in silence, I realized that I did not have a clue about how to meditate.

My Western culture and education, including my theological training, had not prepared me for that moment. I had been made strong in the realm of thought and ideas, but I knew nothing about how to access silent meditation and wordless prayer. This was an important moment for me, the recognition that I knew nothing. In the following days, I received two wonderful gifts: the gift of a dream that carried in Eastern form a message of Love that I had never heard so deeply before and the gift of some simple teaching from a wise old Indian monk at Shantivanam. Through these gifts my soul was opened to learn an ancient form of Eastern meditation that has been foundational to my contemplative life ever since.[11]

> If we pretend that our central trunk is all that we need, if we refuse to grow by sending out secondary roots into the wisdom of other traditions and other nations, we will become not stronger but weaker.

The Spirit was busy those days at Shantivanam, working change in the human heart. Perhaps it is always busy in places that are committed to a true openness of heart and relationship. For Bede Griffiths it was also a time of change. Shortly before I arrived at the ashram, Bede, at the age of eighty-six, had the most transformative experience of his life. During early morning meditation on January 25, 1990, he experienced God as Feminine. For years he had been teaching the marriage of East and West, and the importance of conjoining the feminine and the masculine within ourselves and within our religious images and rituals, but that was in the realm of ideas. This was different. This was an experience of God as Feminine. It shook him down to the foundations of his being. As he later said, "This was too much for my old Western body."

The experience affected him physically, mentally, and spiritually. Physically, it manifested as a stroke, which left him partially paralyzed. Psychologically, it was a moment of illumination. He saw the Feminine as divine. Spiritually, it was an experience of Divine Love. He now realized that everything else was insignificant. A few days after the experience, he wrote to Sister Pascaline Coff at the Osage Monastery in Tulsa, Oklahoma, "The ego has collapsed. I feel totally free. All the barriers have broken down."[12] It was an experience of liberation. He had been set free, not only from his own ego but also from the ego of his Western culture, education, and religious tradition. There were no barriers now. He could give and receive in the utmost openness.

I witnessed the collapse of the ego in my father as he suffered dementia over the last year of his life. It was painful for us as a family to see his loss of memory and words. But, amid the pain, it was also beautiful to see his essence shining through. Like Bede, he experienced the collapse of his individual ego as well as his cultural ego and his religious ego. Nothing tightly contained him anymore. His feelings flowed even more freely than they had earlier in his life. His heart connection with those around him was even more transparent.

I discovered that the people visiting him most frequently were a Muslim couple, Sylvia and Boshe. Years earlier they had escaped from war-torn Bosnia. My father had helped them find sanctuary in Canada. They referred to him as "father" because he had been so central to their birth into freedom and safety. He had always been a deeply compassionate man. This had expressed itself in his work with refugees the world over. But he had also been a very conservative man in his religious beliefs. So, at the end of the day, his feeling toward refugees who belonged to other faiths was that they would be much better off if they became Christian. In other words, his religious ego was pretty big.

The summer before my father died, however, I saw his religious ego dissolving. He always loved to pray with the people visiting him. Somehow, his words would flow when he prayed, even though in ordinary speech he would struggle to find the right words. One beautiful sunny afternoon when we were seated in the garden with Sylvia and Boshe, the summer light dappling through the Canadian maples around us, I asked my father to pray. We were seated in a circle and joined hands. He began his prayer by saying, "Without You, O God, we would not be. And because of You we are one family." I looked across the circle and saw tears streaming down the faces of Boshe and Sylvia. They knew they were one family with us, but they had never heard my father say it. His religious ego had now collapsed. The barriers had broken down.

We are all eventually heading toward that collapse. "Sister Death," as St. Francis calls her in his *Canticle of the Sun*, is coming for each one of us. As frightened as we are of her, she is our sister. She comes in love to free us from our ego—the ego of our nation, our religious tradition, our species, our culture, and our many separatenesses. We will all eventually need to meet her, at the moment of our death. But we do not have to wait until then to get to know her blessings. For it is now that we need to do the work of dying to the way in which our ego claims to be the center, rather than serving the Center. It is now, both individually and collectively, that we need to be freed from the imprisonments that keep us in exile from the true heart of one another.

Finding the Other Half of Our Soul

Over the last five years I have witnessed my second daughter, Kirsten, finding the "other half" of her soul in India. Like Bede, the East awakened her to what she had not discovered in her own homeland. In Kirsten's case, she did not need to do much dying to the ego of Western religion because it had never really claimed her. Through the East, and especially the insights and practices of Hinduism, she was able for the first time in her life to get in touch with the blessings of her Western Christian inheritance.

At Kalakshetra, a dance academy and ashram in Chennai, where she trained in the ancient form of sacred Indian dance known as *bharatanatyam*, the daily pattern was to gather for morning prayer under a great banyan tree at the heart of the ashram. During one of my visits to India, I found it deeply moving to join a hundred young dancers, dressed in their colorful saris and kurtas, seated together at the break of day under the banyan tree chanting prayers from the Hindu, Muslim, and Christian Scriptures. One of the distinctive features of the banyan, an especially sacred tree in India, is the way its branches shoot out in all directions and then, every thirty feet or so, dive back down into the earth to provide secondary roots for the great spreading tree. It is a powerful image of how our great religious traditions, with their strong central trunks can reach out beyond their initial roots to grow and become stronger and provide more and more shelter and sanctuary.

Someone from the United States told me recently that her town in Florida once had many banyan trees growing along its main avenues. The town council, however, decided that they should tidy up the banyans. They were spreading in too many directions. So the town officials ordered all the secondary roots to be cut off. When the next major storm hit Florida, the great banyans were blown over. In losing their secondary roots, they had lost the strength to withstand the storm. So it is, not only in our religious traditions but among us as communities and nations of the world. If we pretend that our central trunk is all that we need, if we refuse to grow by sending out secondary roots into the wisdom of other traditions and other nations, we will become not stronger but weaker.

On our Iona pilgrimage at St. Columba's Bay, each pilgrim picks up two stones. We allow the first stone to represent something that we need to let go of, something that we need to leave behind if we are to move forward in our journey into new beginnings. This may be something in our individual lives, something to which we are clinging unnecessarily, or a regret or failure that is dominating our lives and preventing us from moving forward. Or it may be something in our collective life—in our religion, culture, or nation—an addiction to power or a destructive habit of self-focus that is obstructing our path of new beginnings in the world. We take the first stone and throw it into the sea. We let go of it. We say, No more will this prevent our journey into well-being.

The second stone we allow to represent something for which we are yearning, a new birth that we are longing for in our individual lives or together in our shared life of religion and nationhood. We name within ourselves what that yearning is. We then hold the second stone close to us. We carry it with us from Iona back to our families, our communities, our religious traditions, and our nations. We allow it to be a sign of the new birth for which we are longing.

"Go to the land I will show you," says God to Abram in the Genesis story, and there "I will bless you ... and in you all the families of the earth will be blessed" (Genesis 12:1–3). To truly carry blessing for the world, whether as individuals or together as religious traditions, we are invited to move into new lands of awareness and wisdom. There we will be blessed. And there we will become blessings, for one another and for the families and creatures of the world well beyond the bounds of our own household. "Go to the land I will show you."

Chapter 5

Reconnecting with Spiritual Practice

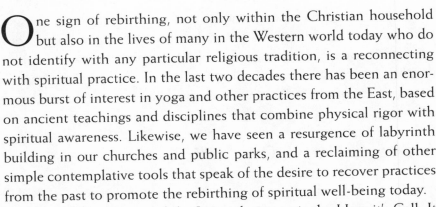

One sign of rebirthing, not only within the Christian household but also in the lives of many in the Western world today who do not identify with any particular religious tradition, is a reconnecting with spiritual practice. In the last two decades there has been an enormous burst of interest in yoga and other practices from the East, based on ancient teachings and disciplines that combine physical rigor with spiritual awareness. Likewise, we have seen a resurgence of labyrinth building in our churches and public parks, and a reclaiming of other simple contemplative tools that speak of the desire to recover practices from the past to promote the rebirthing of spiritual well-being today.

One of the stations of the Iona pilgrimage is the Hermit's Cell. It sits at the heart of the island. No more than a circular ruin of stones, it is the remains of an ancient Celtic beehive hut. Legend has it that Columba and his brothers would retreat there in turn for periods of solitude and prayer as a balance to their life together in community. The Hermit's Cell stands as a sign of the relationship between contemplation and action, silence and expression, solitude and relationship.

On pilgrimage to the Hermit's Cell I was once asked how many monks used to live here—a question that reveals the disorientation

among many moderns in approaching the ancient practices of solitude and stillness. An interesting feature of the Iona Hermit's Cell
is its location. It is hidden amid hills in the interior of the island, so
people often get lost trying to find it. They become disoriented. Similarly, so much of our culture, including our religious inheritance, has
felt lost when it comes to spiritual practice. But we are in the midst of
a reawakening.

One of the things that we remember on pilgrimage as we approach
the Hermit's Cell in silence together is that reclaiming the relationship
between stillness and action, or between solitude and relationship, is
part of the desire to come back into relationship with the wisdom of
nature's rhythms. The earth knows its patterns of night followed by
day, of winter barrenness succeeded by spring energy and summer fruiting, of long periods of infolding and dormancy followed by seasons of
unfolding and the expression of seed-force. We know that if we do not
give ourselves over to the darkness and dreaming of nighttime, entering its intimate invitation to sleep and rest, we will be only half-awake
to the demands and creativity of the day. Yet at other levels we forget
the natural patterns that we are part of. Or we pretend that we can be
deeply engaged and productive while pushing ourselves and others in
ways that are antithetical to the essential rhythms of earth's cycles and
seasons.

A Contemplative Orientation

A great modern Christian prophet of restoring balance through the
disciplines of spiritual practice was Thomas Merton (1915–1968). He
was a Trappist monk from Gethsemani Abbey in Kentucky. Through
his teachings, Merton was not calling us all to a monastic life. He was,
however, inviting us all into what he called a "contemplative orientation" to life.[1] Regardless of our particular vocation, age, stage of life,
marital status, and family commitments, we are invited to find balance—between being and doing, between inner awareness and outward engagement—that will lead to a fuller fruiting of our lives and
relationships.

Merton said, "We are living in a world that is absolutely transparent and God is shining through it all the time ... in people and in things and in nature and in events." But the problem is "We don't see it."[2] Spiritual practice is about remembering to see. It is about intentional disciplines, individually and collectively, that will enable us to be more aware of the shinings of Divine Presence that are within us and all around us. As the Qur'an says, "You have but to remember and you will see the light" (Heights 7:201). It is about training our inner vision to remain alert to the glory that is at the heart of every moment.

For Merton, spiritual practice is not a seeking "to know *about* God" but "to know God."[3] It is a desire for direct personal experience, he says, or existential grasp of the heart of life.[4] The longing that drives the resurgence of spiritual practice today is not a quest for more beliefs about God or for more propositional truths concerning the Almighty. It is the desire to be yoked to the Sacred, which is the root of the Sanskrit word *yoga*. It is the desire to know in the Hebrew Scriptures' sense of the word *yada*, to be intimately joined to the Sacred the way a man and a woman become one in love.

When the nineteenth-century philosopher Friedrich Nietzsche said that God is dead, he was not making an ontological point. He was making an existential point. He was not announcing that God had died, but that our experience of God had died. This was due, in part, to the way in which Western Christianity had focused its attention not on spiritual practice but on spiritual belief. It had confused faith with a set of propositional truths about the Divine, rather than a personal experience of the Divine that could be undergirded and sustained by particular practices and disciplines.

> So much of our culture, including our religious inheritance, has felt lost when it comes to spiritual practice. But we are in the midst of a reawakening.

During my years of leadership at the Abbey on Iona, it was our custom to interview every new volunteer. Volunteers would come from all over the world for periods of seven weeks to join the community's life of prayer and work. So at the beginning of their time we would meet with them individually to welcome them to the vision and commitments of daily life at the Abbey. We would do the same at the end of their time, together reviewing and learning from their experiences in community.

I shall always remember meeting a young volunteer from England named Julie. She wanted to make it clear to me that she was agnostic. She understood that morning and evening prayer were part of our daily rhythm at the Abbey—and that she was expected to participate in this aspect of community life—but she wanted me to know that she had no religious belief. I respected her forthrightness and willingness to take on the full range of commitments. I often noticed Julie during her tenure at the Abbey, working hard in the housekeeping department and showing up for prayer. At the end of her seven weeks, we met again to do a review. When I asked her what had been the most memorable aspect of her time on the island, she said it had been communal prayer in the Abbey. "I am still agnostic," she said, "but I really loved morning prayer."

As Merton says, spiritual practice is not about an idea or concept of God. It is about seeking the experience of presence.[5] What Julie had experienced in morning prayer was a sense of presence. What was important was not her idea or concept of God. It was her existential accessing of something at the heart of life. Being in touch with that something at the heart of life affected the way she lived her life. Julie has remained in touch with us over the years. I have not questioned her about theological beliefs lately, but my guess is that she is still more interested in knowing than knowing *about*, in experiencing the Essence rather than holding particular beliefs about the Essence. In this I do not believe she is alone. I believe Julie expresses the search that is widespread, the growing desire to experience the Sacred.

At the age of eighty-four, Carl Jung was interviewed about his life journey. The interview included recollections of some of his earliest moments of consciousness as a little boy when, amid the trees and growing things, what he most wanted to do, he said, was "crawl into the essence of nature."[6] In the interview Jung was asked if he believed in God, to which he responded, "I don't need to believe. I know."[7] This was not an arrogant response. Jung was not claiming to know in an intellectual sense. Over his long life in psychoanalytical work, he had learned to crawl into the very essence of life, into the heart of the human mystery. In that way he had experienced the Essence. He knew it firsthand. And that was what was most important to Jung, rather than believing particular things about the Essence. This, I believe, expresses the yearning at the heart of the rebirth of spiritual practice today, the yearning to experientially touch the Center.

During my time at the Abbey on Iona, I was given a study leave to do some writing on the Greek island of Patmos in the Aegean Sea. Patmos is where John the Beloved lived for many years in political exile during the latter half of the first century CE, probably because he was related to the family of Jesus, which the Roman Empire feared, just as they had feared Jesus and his brothers in their radical association with the poor and powerless of Palestine. I was staying in a little guest house under the shadow of the Monastery of St. John.

There, over the garden wall, I met Peter France, who had been a television presenter for the BBC series *Everyman*. One evening as we sipped ouzo together, Peter told me the story of how he had arrived on Patmos years earlier to do a series on Eastern Orthodoxy. His own background was secular. He had been reared in a British family of strong socialist principles but with no formal religious belief. Halfway through the filming of the documentary, he had a spiritual experience that changed his vision of reality, and he decided to become a Greek Orthodox Christian.

> As Merton says, spiritual practice is not about an idea or concept of God. It is about seeking the experience of presence.

Peter was assigned a monk from the monastery to guide him toward baptism. They met on a regular basis to explore the history and practices of Greek Orthodoxy. As they approached Easter and the time of baptism, the monk explained to him what would happen in the liturgy and what he would be expected to do and say during the baptismal service. At that point, Peter realized he was going to be asked to give intellectual assent to the fourth-century propositional statements about God in the Nicene Creed. He explained to the monk that he did not feel it would be authentic for him to declare his belief in these statements. These creedal statements *about* God, which are still recited weekly in Christian churches throughout the world, were not something that represented his experience *of* God. So in the following weeks they wrestled together with the meaning of this ancient text of inherited belief. In the end Peter said he could not proceed. At that point the monk said, "Don't worry, Peter. I will say the words of the Creed for you."

The monk had clearly seen the purity of Peter's heart. He saw the beauty of the experience of the Sacred that had led to Peter's desire to practice Orthodox spirituality. Most wisely of all, he saw that a statement of propositional belief about God should not stand in the way of Peter's journey of faith. There is a place for attempting to articulate what we believe about God and to do this together in the context of past articulations and Christianity's unfolding history of beliefs. But these definitions of faith should be kept on the back shelves of the Christian family's library and not by the front door as a requirement for entry. The training of our priests and ministers in the Christian tradition needs to give as much attention to spiritual practice as it has to religious belief. For it is spiritual practice that will again and again enable us to experience the Sacred at the heart of life in ways that will shape how we live and undergird how we work to heal the world.

Finding Our Diamond Essence

In Merton's teachings on spiritual practice we can discern a threefold pattern. The first is his belief that spiritual practice is about remembering our diamond essence.[8] It is about remembering that what is deepest in us is of God. The second is his conviction that spiritual practice is about remembering that that diamond essence is at the heart of each one of us and of all things. The third is his belief that we will find true strength for the holy work of transformation in the world only by digging deep into the foundations of our being. Enduring strength will be found not in our ego but in our essence.

Merton's first emphasis is that what is deepest in us is like "pure diamond, blazing with the invisible light of heaven."[9] In spiritual practice we return to this deepest center.[10] In meditation, he says, we penetrate the innermost ground of our life.[11] This allows us to find our true meaning not from the *outside*, he says, but from *within*.[12] It means that we identify ourselves not in terms of social status, race, religion, or sexual orientation but by our truest identity in the very ground of our being.

My own religious upbringing did not provide me with a strong sense of this innermost ground, nor did it offer me contemplative practices. But there was much in me, just as I believe there is much in every child, that was naturally contemplative. I was a dreamy boy. Many of my earliest recollections are of gazing with a type of open-eyed wonder at the universe, at the dewdrops of moisture in the morning grass, at the summer sunlight shimmering off the pure waters of northern Canadian lakes, and at night, by those same lakes, being almost mesmerized as I watched the shinings of heaven's infinity. I was so filled with a type of natural contemplation of the world's dreamlikeness that I was extremely slow to speak. I was too busy listening and watching.

> It is spiritual practice that will again and again enable us to experience the Sacred at the heart of life in ways that will shape how we live and undergird how we work to heal the world.

The first time I formally accessed spiritual practice came during my college years through contact with the Taize community. This is an ecumenical monastic community in France that had its origins in providing shelter during the Second World War for French Jews hiding from Nazi persecution. One of the gifts of the Taize community was the way it had reclaimed ancient contemplative practice from early Christianity to make it accessible for today, particularly the use of chant based on a simple repetition of words from Scripture.

My wife and I had just become engaged. I look back with great fondness on the way in which we would kneel side by side in the mornings and read simple prayers from the Taize community and particularly how we would chant together. There was a purity and even innocence to our newfound spiritual practice. We were like novices.

Merton says we may not want to be seen as beginners in spiritual practice. "But let us be convinced of the fact that we will never be anything else but beginners, all our life!"[13] The first people to acknowledge this are usually those who are most committed to the spiritual disciplines of silence, meditation, and mindfulness. In my work with groups across the Western world, I notice in our meditation practices together that, nearly always, each of the participants thinks that everyone else is doing a better job meditating than they are. Let us name this misconception for what it is. We are all given to distraction and to the discomforts of body and disruptions of thought that keep taking us away from the Center and from a deep remembering of the diamond essence that is at our core.

> It speaks of the new monasticism to which we are being called, not closed in or cut off from the earth and the struggles of the world but open both to the glory and the brokenness that are in all things.

While we were discovering the Taize community, Ali and I were drawn into relationship with a contemplative community just outside Edinburgh, the Community of the Transfiguration, as it was then known. They lived a life of utter simplicity. Each monk had a garden shed in which to sleep, and together they shared a main house that was used primarily for hospitality. There they welcomed anyone and everyone who arrived on their doorstep, ranging from refined English bishops to hardened Scottish men of the road.

The chapel at the Community of the Transfiguration was a simple structure of two garden huts joined together. At one end was a little altar with icons on the wall. Along the side walls were benches that could seat up to five people each. We would chant antiphonally: "O

God, make speed to save us" by those on one side; "O Lord, make haste to help us" by those on the opposite side. Back and forth, back and forth, we would chant, working our way through Psalms and Scripture Canticles. The memory of this lingers with me like the sweet smell of incense, which the community also used in prayer. But primarily what I remember is the simple practice of presence. Deeper than words, deeper than thought and belief, we were reaching into the Presence.

Part of the beauty of the Community of the Transfiguration was that the monks did not take themselves too seriously or inflate the significance of their religiosity. After evening prayer in the garden chapel, sitting together in the main house, Brother Roland would say with a twinkle in his eye, "The problem with heaven is that we'll have to spend all of our time with God." This prompted great bursts of laughter. It was Roland who taught us that there are two types of prayer. One, he said, is the dozing pussycat prayer, purring by the warm fire of God's presence. The other is the yappy dog prayer, scratching at the door of heaven, imploring God's help in our lives.

Maybe we need both. But contemplative prayer, as Merton said, "is essentially a listening in silence, an expectancy."[14] It is always very simple "often making use of no words and no thoughts at all."[15] Echoing that thought, the Scottish poet Edwin Muir (1887–1959) says, the problem with truth is not that it is too complicated for expression. It is too simple for expression, "too deep for daily tongues to say."[16] The simpler we can be in our expressions and practices, including our spiritual practices, the closer we will come to the Truth and to our diamond essence.

Merton said that spiritual practice could be described as a "preference for the desert," for the stripped-down place, for the settings and disciplines that allow us to move more readily into the elemental spaces of our inner landscape.[17] It is no coincidence, I believe, that Merton's mother was a Quaker. Though she died when he was only six years old, the traces of her spirituality, with its love of silence and its seeking the inner light at the heart of life, are strong in Merton's later writings and teachings. To know God is to know our essence. And to know our essence is to know God. He was fond of quoting St. Augustine: *"Noverim te noverim me*—May I know You, may I know myself."[18] To move toward the light that is within us, "the Light that enlightens every person coming into the world" (John 1:9, adapted), is to move toward the Holy.

Plunging Deep into the Heart of the World

Merton's second emphasis is that spiritual practice is about remembering the diamond essence in everybody and in everything.[19] "There is in all visible things an invisible fecundity," he said, "an inexhaustible sweetness" that flows to us "from the unseen roots of all created being."[20] The glory that we access at the heart of our own being through spiritual practice is at the heart of all being.

For almost ten years now, my wife and I have been spending part of every summer at Casa del Sol (House of the Sun), a center for contemplation and retreat in New Mexico. An old hacienda on the grounds of Ghost Ranch Conference Center, Casa del Sol sits in its own open space below the mesas three miles farther out into the desert, just along the road from where the great American artist Georgia O'Keefe lived and painted. So its context is that wild expansiveness of high desert landscape that we associate with O'Keefe's paintings and their sensuous invitation into the heart of flowers that unexpectedly blossom in barren desert.

In the summers at Casa del Sol, all of our teaching and meditation happens outside. The traditional hacienda architecture means that the courtyard is surrounded on three sides by the main wings of the house. It feels almost like a cloister. But very importantly there is no fourth side. It is not closed in. Our meditations and reflections feel supported by the structure of the building. Its north-south wings are like two arms holding us securely, at times allowing us to experience communally an unusual intimacy of sharing and tears. But the fourth side of the courtyard opens out onto the vastness of the high desert. For me it is an image of how true spiritual practice opens into relationship with all things. It speaks of the new monasticism to which we are being called, not closed in or cut off from the earth and the struggles of the world but open both to the glory and the brokenness that are in all things.

Merton says that "the monk searches not only his own heart: he plunges deep into the heart of that world of which he remains a part although he seems to have 'left' it."[21] Spiritual practice is not only about moving to the diamond center of our own being. It is about plunging deep into the heart of the world. Merton had not always been clear about this in his monastic journey. His classic piece on the monastic life, *The Seven Story Mountain*, first published in 1948 and read by hundreds of thousands over the years, was at times condescending in tone, giving the impression that the cloistered life of the monk was the ideal to which all other spiritual practices should strive. But even by 1951, three years after its publication, Merton said of the book, this is "the work of a man I never even heard of."[22] He was ashamed at its arrogance. In his next major publication he wrote, "I have come to the monastery to find my place in the world and if I fail to find this place in the world, I will be wasting my time in the monastery."[23] Moving deep into the heart of all things is an essential feature of authentic spiritual practice.

This feature of Merton's spiritual life increasingly came to the fore over the following years, and in 1958 he had an experience that confirmed and deepened it. He had been in Louisville, Kentucky, meeting with his publisher. Afterward, at the corner of Fourth and Walnut Streets, as he walked through the shopping district of the city, he was suddenly overwhelmed by the realization that he loved everyone around him, "that they were mine and I theirs, that we could not be alien to one another even though we were total strangers. It was like waking from a dream of separateness."[24] He saw the "secret beauty of their heart." It was as if they were all walking around shining like the sun. "If only we could see each other that way all the time," he wrote. "There would be no more war, no more hatred, no more cruelty, no more greed.... I suppose the big problem would be that we would fall down and worship each other."[25]

This, in a sense, is exactly what happened to Merton some years later. Having awakened from the "dream of separateness" that had clouded his vision, he met and fell in love with a young woman named Margie Smith, a student nurse in Louisville who had cared for him while he was in the hospital. To him, she was the embodiment of Lady Wisdom. He saw in her that "inexhaustible sweetness" that rises up from the root of life, and he longed to taste that sweetness in her. This led to a confusing time in his life. He had to decide whether he would continue to make his offering to the world through the monastic path of commitment or through a new commitment—his relationship with Margie. In the end, Merton decided to continue his monastic vocation.

When we see the secret beauty in another's heart, when we see that person walking around shining like the sun, we face the problem that Merton became aware of that afternoon in 1958 at the corner of Fourth and Walnut—wanting to fall down and worship the other. He had to wrestle with that problem in 1966 in his relationship with Margie Smith. But the real problem that we need to face in our lives and our world is not the struggle of what we do when we fall in love with another. This is not to diminish the reality of such struggles and the need for discernment at such moments. But the real problem that overwhelmingly confronts most of us in the world most of the time is that we are not falling in love with the heart of one another and the heart of other nations and species. We are blind to their secret beauty; thus, we fail even to be tempted to fall down and worship them.

> Spiritual practice is about being turned completely inside out. It is to discover that our true center is the Self at the heart of one another.

This is the problem that spiritual practice sets out to address. As Merton wrote around the same time in his life, when people are in love, "They are more than their everyday selves, more alive, more understanding, more enduring.... They are made over into new beings."[26] After his epiphany on the streets of downtown Louisville, Merton began to plow his energies into relationships with some of the leading peace activists of the day. Joan Baez and Daniel Berrigan could be found visiting him in his hermitage. He corresponded with Martin Luther King Jr. about the civil rights movement. Also during these years he forged close relationships with the leaders of other religious traditions, the Dalai Lama, Thich Nhat Hanh (b. 1926), and the Zen scholar D. T. Suzuki (1870–1966). The deepest ground of our being, he said, cries out for communion.[27] The unity for which we long, he said, is not a new unity. It is our original unity.[28] We do not have to create our relationship with all things. We simply need to let it be born again from the very foundations of our being. Spiritual practice is at the heart of this great work.

Nurturing the Seed-Force for Change

Merton's third emphasis in spiritual practice focuses on accessing the diamond essence of our being in order to be strong for the work of transformation in the world. This involves dying to the way in which the ego wants to be the center, whether that be our individual ego or our collective ego—the ego of our nation, religious tradition, or species. As Jesus said, "Unless a grain of wheat falls into the earth and dies, it remains just a single grain; but if it dies, it bears much fruit" (John 12:24). Our seed-force of strength for change in the world will multiply by accessing the innermost ground of our being. That is where true strength is to be found, not in the limited strength of the ego.

This, says Merton, involves facing our nothingness in order to access our everythingness.[29] It means facing the worst in us in order to discover the best.[30] It means we need to "die on a certain level of our being in order to find ourselves alive and free at another."[31] This does not involve a hatred of the self. And it certainly does not require us to demean the self in others, or in other races, classes, and genders. Quite the opposite. It means respecting the self and nurturing it in others. This includes our children and those among us who have not been fully respected or have been given the impression they have nothing to offer. But part of truly respecting the self is remembering that we are not God. In and by ourselves we are nothing. Yet within us is everything. The important role of the ego is to become conscious of the true ground of our being and to promote the liberation of these depths, rather than forgetting or neglecting these depths.

This work of inner change, dying at a certain level in order to live at another, is essential.[32] Without it, says Merton, there can be no peace because without it we end up defining ourselves in terms of our ego, whether individually or collectively.[33] We end up defending the small self in its separateness rather than the Self within all selves. To truly respect the Self involves deeply respecting the small self and our distinct individualities, but it does not involve inflating our small self. Spiritual practice, says Merton, is about being turned completely inside out.[34] It is to discover that our true center is the Self at the heart of one another and that we will be truly well only to the extent that we treat the other as we treat ourself.

This work need not be mournful, says Merton.[35] It is essentially liberating. Think of the joy in the men and women of greatest spiritual stature in our world today—the Dalai Lama, Archbishop Desmond Tutu (b. 1931), Aung San Suu Kyi of Burma. They have been set free from what Merton calls the "intolerable burden of self-important seriousness."[36] They have discovered that we are most free when we do not lift ourselves up over one another but when we remember that our true Center is at the heart of one another.

One of the last times I visited the Hermit's Cell on Iona was with my family. Rather than leading a group of pilgrims, I was with relatives, including two of my children and several nieces and nephews. Rather than being revered as an internationally renowned teacher of spirituality, I was being treated endearingly as the object of some loving ridicule that comes with being the paterfamilias. Among those on hand for the visit were a niece and a nephew who, knowing my regard for spiritual practice, had named one of their hens back home Thomas Merton, a bit of humor that I am pretty sure Merton would have loved. When we arrived at the Hermit's Cell, where I often lead pilgrims in a simple tai chi sequence, I decided that I should offer the same to my family, and they agreed. So there we stood in a circle—some of us explicitly religious in our beliefs, others explicitly irreligious, and still others who would not have even given religion or spirituality a single thought—and amid smiles and reverent laughter we shared some simple tai chi movements. I would say that we became a little stronger together at that moment, a little fonder of one another, and a little bit more aware of something deeper than us all.

Spiritual practice is not about self-important seriousness. Rather, it is about doing something that Merton says is both less serious and more serious—a Cosmic Dance in which we discover that we do not have to take the lead.[37] We cannot take the lead for we do not know how to. But we can give ourselves to the Dance. We can let go with abandon to it, to be carried by its endless rhythm in a relationship that is deeper than our consciousness can comprehend. But what is most serious about the Dance is that each one of us is needed. There is a place in the Dance of the Universe that no one else can take but each of us.

Merton died suddenly and unexpectedly on December 10, 1968, at the age of fifty-three. We do not know what he was thinking at the last moment, but we do know that in his lifetime he had come to believe that precisely at the point of dying to the ego we encounter God's fullness.[38] It is precisely when the ego lets go of having to be in control that we can receive the universe's gifts most fully. We do know that he believed that the important work of spiritual practice is to access that fullness now for the sake of one another and for the world. This is the work that will be at the heart of a new rebirthing.

Chapter 6

Reconnecting with Nonviolence

The rebirthing of God is about what is deepest in us coming forth again. It is about our sacred depths being born afresh in radically new ways. A prominent feature of this rebirthing is nonviolence, the refusal to use violent force against one another in our relationships as individuals, as nations, and as a species. It is about reclaiming nonviolence as the deepest and truest energy for creating and sustaining peaceful change in the world.

Dun I is the highest point on Iona. We approach it in pilgrimage from the Hermit's Cell. Dun I simply means the hill of I, or the hill of Iona. From the summit we can see the entire island and, on a clear day, over sixty miles in every direction, taking in the Cuillins of Skye to the north, the Paps of Jura to the southeast, and vast stretches of open Atlantic Ocean to the west. It is a magnificent view. On pilgrimage we reflect on the importance of perspective in our lives and our world, of seeing all things in relationship. Included in this perspective from Dun I is the White Strand of the Monks, a white sandy beach at the northeast corner of Iona where, in 806 CE, sixty-eight monks were slaughtered at the hands of Norse invaders.

This island of peace has experienced its share of violence and bloodshed. It is not cut off from the places of deep wrongdoing and suffering in our world, where injustice and war are tearing apart the fabric of whole communities and nations. Yet Iona, a holy site of pilgrimage, has always been associated with peacemaking. Its great sixth-century saint, Columba, was revered as a prophet of peace. His name in Gaelic, Columcille, means "dove of the church." Yet the vision for peacemaking that has been nurtured in this place over the centuries is grounded in an awareness and experience of the violence that humanity is capable of.

Response-Ability

This same combination of passion for peace and sharp sensitivity to the conflicts and violence of our world also characterized Iona's twentieth-century prophet, George MacLeod (1895–1991). As we have already noted, he was the founder of the modern-day Iona community in Scotland and was deeply committed to the vision and practice of nonviolence. So much so that those who remember meeting him, whether on the busy streets of Edinburgh or along the quiet pathways of Iona, also remember that he would often begin his conversations not with the normal pleasantry of "Hello, how are you?" but with the challenging question "Do you believe in nonviolence?" He would ask it with such assertive presence that you felt afraid to say no. MacLeod was, without a doubt, the most aggressive pacifist the modern world has known.

But he would not always begin his conversations with challenge. Sometimes he led with humor. His other favorite starting point in conversation was to ask, "Are you a Presbyterian or a Christian?" which, in Presbyterian Scotland, was to amusingly raise an unheard-of question. But, whether it was with the passion of challenge or the playfulness of banter, you always knew in meeting George MacLeod that you would not feel as comfortable at the end of the conversation as you did at the beginning. This, of course, is the role of the prophet, in both word and action—to raise questions about how we view ourselves and about the assumptions by which we live and act.

MacLeod had not always been a pacifist. He grew up in an aristocratic Scottish family. His father was Sir John MacLeod, a respected political establishment figure. His family home had domestic staff and printed menus for evening meals. He attended Winchester College, one of the most exclusive schools for boys in Britain, before going on to university at Oriel College in Oxford. He then became an officer in the British army and saw action at the Battle of Ypres in 1917, for which he was decorated with the Croix de Guerre, France's highest military honor for bravery.

But a turning point came toward the end of the war when he was traveling by train close to the front lines. The railway carriage was filled with soldiers, some of whom had been wounded in conflict. It was here that MacLeod experienced the presence of Christ, not as separate from the woundedness and struggle all around him, but within the brokenness and the pain. MacLeod, always a man of action, immediately knelt down where he was, surrounded by his fellow soldiers in the crowded train car, and gave himself to Christ.

After the war he trained for the Church of Scotland ministry. During these years he increasingly began to see the connection between commitment to the way of Christ and commitment to peacemaking. No longer a soldier of the British army, MacLeod now spoke of himself as a *Miles Christi*, a solider of Christ. To follow Christ was to follow Christ's way, the way of nonviolence.

He soon became a rising star in the Church of Scotland. After training theologically, MacLeod was appointed assistant minister at St. Giles in Edinburgh, Scotland's national cathedral, and was widely acclaimed for his gift of preaching. His public prayers, which would take only a few minutes to deliver, were carefully and poetically crafted for hours to convey, in distilled form, the essence of his vision. It soon became clear that he could have his choice of pulpits in Scotland. But he surprised everyone by accepting a call to one of the poorest parishes in the nation, Govan Old in Glasgow, characterized in the early 1930s by massive unemployment.

Here, as MacLeod toiled amid the poverty and social inequities of early twentieth-century Scotland, he began to dream of rebuilding the Abbey on Iona as a sign of recovering the spirituality of Columba, the prophet of peace. In 1938 the reconstruction began—MacLeod leading ministers, students, and unemployed craftsmen in building a vision that in years to come would inspire the hearts and minds of thousands of Christians around the world to reclaim peacemaking as essential to the way of following Christ.

In a prayer from the rebuilding days, MacLeod wrote:

> It is not just the interior of these walls,
> it is our own inner beings You [are renewing] ...
> We are Your temple not made with hands.
> We are Your body.
> If every wall should crumble, and every church decay,
> we are Your habitation ...
> We bless You for this place ...
> [but] take us "outside the camp," Lord,
> outside holiness,
> out to where soldiers gamble,
> and thieves curse,
> and nations clash
> at the cross-roads of the world....
> So shall this building continue to be justified.[1]

Prayer was not unrelated to political engagement. Spirituality was not separate from peacemaking. Rebuilding the Abbey on Iona was not unconnected to the health of nations. MacLeod preached whole salvation, as he liked to say, rather than simply soul salvation. The great offering of Christ to humanity was not about salvation *from* the world. It was about salvation *of* the world. Jesus showed a way of transformation from the injustices and violence that dominate the world of international relations and domestic affairs.

I first met George MacLeod on Iona in 1979. I was a young student. He, by that stage, was in his early eighties. I had already heard him speak publicly in Edinburgh and had been deeply moved. It struck me then like coming home, to hear a Christian teacher who believed in the sacredness of the earth and taught nonviolence. But we had not yet met. And here suddenly, on an Iona footpath, my wife and I bumped into the great man. He invited us back to where he was staying on the island, for a whiskey!

I was not accustomed to drinking whiskey, and certainly not in the midafternoon. But when a legend invites you for whiskey, you go for whiskey. At the house we found Lorna, his wife, equally formidable and nearly always energetically disagreeing with George. They were like good sparring partners. Ali and Lorna fell into conversation on one side of the room, and on the other side George and I began to speak about peacemaking and caring for the earth. What I shall always remember from that first conversation was MacLeod saying to me toward the end of our discussion, "Newell, what are we going to do about all this?"

Looking back on that question, I realize the words that deeply struck me were *we* and *do*. What are *we* going to *do* about this? He could so easily have said, "Let me tell you, young man," but he didn't. One of his great gifts as a leader, especially of young men, was to allow us to share his vision, to claim it for ourselves, and to act on it. He taught that we have the ability to respond to the injustices and violence of our nations and our world. We have response-ability. Will we accept it? This was forever MacLeod's challenging question.

> This is the role of the prophet, in both word and action— to raise questions about how we view ourselves and about the assumptions by which we live and act.

Love-Force Not Brute-Force

Around the same time as George MacLeod's life-changing experience of Christ on the front lines during World War I, Mahatma Gandhi (1869–1948), the modern world's greatest prophet of nonviolence, was leading a movement called *satyagraba* (truth-force) in a thirty-year struggle to free India, nonviolently, from British domination.

Gandhi has been hailed as the twentieth century's most Christ-like figure. Interestingly, of course, he was not a Christian. He was a Hindu. But the only picture he had in his room at the Sabarmati Ashram in Ahmedabad showed Jesus with an inscription below that read "He is our Peace."[2] Gandhi called Jesus the great "Asian prophet," a reminder to the West that our central figure of religious belief was not a Westerner at all.[3] As Gandhi used to say, if Christians had actually done what Jesus taught us to do—namely, love our enemy—the world would long ago have been transformed. "Christianity became disfigured when it went to the West," said Gandhi. "It became the religion of kings."[4] Gandhi challenged us to turn our creed back into deed, our belief in Jesus into following the practice of Jesus.

In India's long struggle for self-rule, Gandhi believed it was not enough to simply defeat the British. The goal was to turn the fiends of India into the friends of India, to transform the relationship between nations, not simply to overthrow the British. "I refuse to regard anyone as my enemy," said Gandhi.[5] Hatred of the other can never lead to true liberation. So Gandhi distinguished between two kinds of force. There is brute-force, he said, and there is love-force.[6] There is the use of violence against an oppressor and there is the use of active noncooperation or civil disobedience. The latter is "a thousand times more effective" than the former.[7] He believed that an eye for an eye would only make the whole world blind. On the other hand, love-force, or soul-force as he also called it, can change the heart and the will of an entire nation.[8]

> The great offering of Christ to humanity was not about salvation *from* the world. It was about salvation *of* the world.

Gandhi was immensely creative in his use of truth-force. In the Salt March of 1930 he led thousands of Indians on a 240-mile walk to the sea to produce their own salt as a symbolic gesture in opposition to the British Raj, which held a monopoly on the production and taxation of salt. The Salt March sparked widespread action across the whole of India, in which millions of Indians participated in acts of civil disobedience. It also attracted newspaper and newsreel coverage, leading to international criticism of the way in which British police were beating nonviolent participants in the Salt March. Gandhi had begun to change the hearts of Britons and countless others throughout the world.

A major feature of the rebirthing of soul-force is action that is guided by creativity, rather than by the thoughtless counteraction of violence with violence. "Counter-hatred," Gandhi said, "only increases the surface as well as the depth of hatred."[9] For him the end never justifies the means. Wrong must never be used to combat wrong. Or, as the Christian Scriptures teach and Gandhi often quoted, "Overcome evil with good" (Romans 12:21). He believed that the methods employed in any attempt to confront injustice must reflect the spirit of the goal. That is, true action for change must be guided by the spirit of love.

Many years ago I was asked to lead a retreat at a Roman Catholic convent in the south of England. When I arrived, the mother superior welcomed me warmly and insisted that I join in every aspect of their community life together. Part of what she was saying to me, of course, was that even though I was a Protestant I should feel entirely free to receive the bread and wine at Mass.

"Normally we have Father Peter presiding," she said. "Poor Father Peter. He doesn't have the use of his arms, so when he presides at communion one of the sisters does the actions and he says the words. Poor Father Peter. But this Sunday we have Father John," she continued. "Poor Father John. He doesn't have the use of his voice so when he celebrates one of the sisters says the words and he does the actions. Poor Father John."

This was a wise old mother. Clearly she had arranged only for priests with some physical limitation to preside. It meant that the experience of communion at the convent felt like concelebration, a conjoining of feminine and masculine leadership. This was being creative. It was combating the wrong of male domination in her tradition not with angry protest at the holders of ecclesiastical power but with the ingenuity of love or what Gandhi called the "arts of love."[10] "Hate the sin but not the sinner," he said.[11]

By noncooperation Gandhi did not mean passive resistance or doing nothing in the face of injustice. Truth-force calls for both creativity and the courage to speak out. "It is as necessary to reject untruth as it is to accept truth," he said.[12] There is in English a "very potent word," taught Gandhi, and "all the languages of the world have it—it is 'No.'"[13]

No, we will not tolerate one nation dominating another! No, we will not accept a system in which some are treated with dignity and others with disrespect! No, we will not employ violent means to attain peace! No! No! No! A most powerful word. But for Gandhi it was inextricably linked to an even more fundamental word: Yes. Yes, to the true heart of every nation! Yes, to the essential sacredness of every human being! Yes, to the power of truth-force! The *no* that we must speak and live in our lives in the face of wrongdoing needs to be based on a deeper *yes*, a radical affirmation of the sacred core of every human being.

Gandhi, a faithful Indian Hindu, regarded the Muslims and Christians of his nation as blood brothers and sisters.[14] They were part of him and he was part of them. They belonged together in relationship as a single family. He said, "I am a Hindu and a Christian and a Muslim and a Jew."[15] This was not to downplay the importance and uniqueness of his Hinduism. Rather, it was to accentuate his respect for the other great religious traditions of India. He needed them to complete his Hinduism. "I broaden my Hinduism by loving other religions as my own," said Gandhi.[16] As he said to Indian Christians who shared the religion of the British Empire, your innermost prayer should be to make Hindus better Hindus, not to make them Christian.[17] Our religious inheritances are given to bless the world, not to convert the world. "We have but one soul," he said. "The rays of the sun are many through refraction. But they have the same source."[18]

Love Is the Strongest Yet Humblest Force

How do we access soul-force? Where do we find the strength to live nonviolently in our lives and our world? For Gandhi it was through prayer and meditation. Prayer "has saved my life," he said.[19] "As food is necessary for the body, prayer is necessary for the soul."[20] It is through daily spiritual practice that we can be renewed in our true depths. The sacred ground from which soul-force arises is deep within. This is not to say that we will only encounter truth in the inner chambers of our being. There we will meet not only angels of light but also angels of darkness, messengers of fear and pride. In Gandhi's journey he was aware of wrestling with all of these within himself. "The Inner Voice may mean a message from God or from the Devil," he said. The action that follows determines "the nature of the Voice."[21]

During my years serving the Anglican Diocese of Portsmouth in England, I got to know a Roman Catholic priest named David. He was passionate about peacemaking and about the work of justice that undergirds true relationship in our lives and our world. For many years he had given himself to the poorest and most powerless of Portsmouth. He was a renowned and popular figure throughout the city, so much so that despite his often radical and unorthodox ways the bishop was reluctant to rein him in. This was further complicated by the fact that David was gay and lived openly with his partner, a Zen Buddhist.

David invited Ali and me to lead a series on spirituality at his church. But before the series he said we should come some Sunday morning simply to get to know the community a little. The Sunday we attended services was

> A major feature of the rebirthing of soul-force is action that is guided by creativity, rather than by the thoughtless counteraction of violence with violence.

the World Day of Prayer for Peace. David gave a passionate homily on nonviolence. We then moved into the celebration of communion. Although little children had been running around during the homily, free to come and go from their families, they were now pulled back into the pews by their parents to sit attentively for the sacrament. But the problem was that Ali and I had not noticed this soon enough. Our little Cameron, age three, was still clattering along the wooden bench next to us with hard-heeled shoes on. At which point a woman on the far side of the church shouted out, "Would someone keep that child quiet."

David did not realize who was being referred to but, having just started the celebration of communion, he stopped and said, "Claudia, if that is how you feel, leave." To which the woman named Claudia responded, "But Father, I couldn't hear the words of the liturgy." Turning a little red with frustration, David replied, "We have been building a community here that is inclusive of every person and every age. So, Claudia, if that is how you feel, leave." At this point the congregation was highly attentive. This was real drama in the midst of formal liturgy. But they did not look worried. This was just a good family argument.

But Claudia spoke a third time and this time David, by now bright red in the face, slammed his hands down on the altar and left the raised dais, heading straight for Claudia. Seeing fire in David's eyes, his Buddhist partner leapt up and tried to stop him from proceeding down the aisle. The family argument had now become a wrestling match! Finally, David reached Claudia, who, as it turned out, had been one of his earliest and staunchest supporters. So it was with real puzzlement in his voice that David asked her, "Claudia, what are you saying?"

> There are angels of light and angels of darkness in us all. One moment we may be preaching nonviolence as the only true energy for real transformation in our world. The next moment we may be consumed by violence of heart.

Claudia left in tears, followed by a few members of the congregation to console her. Then David returned to the altar and said, "I cannot proceed until I ask for forgiveness. I do not apologize for defending the place of children, but I do apologize for my violence of heart. I was wrong. I ask God's forgiveness and I will seek Claudia's forgiveness." He then proceeded with the celebration and before the end of the liturgy Claudia was back to receive the bread and wine from the hands of David. The family fight was over.

There are angels of light and angels of darkness in us all. One moment we may be preaching nonviolence as the only true energy for real transformation in our world. The next moment we may be consumed by violence of heart. Sometimes this is provoked by the most trivial of disagreements and at other times by differences of real substance. But whether or not our violent feelings or actions ever feel justified, that is never the place from which we can effect real change if we are seeking peace. That is why Gandhi taught that it is through prayer and meditation that we access true strength. Our prayer, he said, "must be combined with the utmost humility."[22] It must be accompanied by the radical awareness of knowing that soul-force is not the possession of our ego. It is the property of our innermost being. "Love is the strongest force the world possesses and yet it is the humblest imaginable."[23]

Gandhi concludes his autobiographical work *My Experiments with Truth* by saying, "I must reduce myself to zero."[24] This was not self-hatred in Gandhi. He knew how colorful his personality was, and he knew just how effectively it could be brought to bear in India's great push for liberation. But, most importantly, he knew that he would have no deep resources for the struggle to liberate his nation from British rule if he drew only from his ego strength. This is not where soul-force comes from. It comes from the very ground of our being, from that place within us all, the Soul within all souls, the Life at the heart of all life. Unless our ego is strong and secure enough to do the essential work of dying to the way in which it wants to be the center, we will obstruct the flow of soul-force, not promote it.

Gandhi was assassinated on his way to evening prayer on January 30, 1948. He was killed by one of his own, a Hindu who feared that Gandhi's vision of family unity between Hindus and Muslims would lead to too much power being ceded to the Muslim minority in independent India. But the fear behind this violent act of assassination had no true place in Hinduism. It was driven by religious fundamentalism's refusal to open the boundaries of the human heart. It was rooted in the fear that Gandhi could not protect his Hindu brothers and sisters and at the same time be true to the Muslim community of India. He could not both love the one and respect the other; thus occurred the tragic violence that killed a great prophet and divided a nation.

Blessed Are the Peacemakers

When Gandhi was assassinated, George MacLeod was still re-forming a vision of nonviolence for Scotland amid the rebuilding of Iona Abbey. As usual, his prayers reflected his passion for peace:

> Sun behind all suns,
> Soul behind all souls,
>
> .....
>
> Show to us in everything we touch and in everyone we meet
> the continued assurance of Thy presence round us:
> lest ever we should think Thee absent.
> In all created things Thou art there.
> In every friend we have
> the sunshine of Thy presence is shown forth.
> In every enemy that seems to cross our path,
> Thou art there within the cloud
> to challenge us to love.
> Show to us the glory in the grey.
> Awake for us Thy presence in the very storm
> till all our joys are seen as Thee
> and all our trivial tasks emerge as priestly sacraments
> in the universal temple of Thy love.[25]

Hidden in all things, even in the heart of the enemy, is the Sacred Presence challenging us to love.

Like Gandhi, MacLeod too had brothers and sisters in his own religious household who feared and hated him. How could he both love his enemy—in that era the Soviet Union—and truly care for his own nation? How could he enter into relationship with leaders of the Roman Catholic Church and truly lead his own Protestant tradition? Despite many detractors, MacLeod was also well-loved. In 1957 he became moderator of the General Assembly, the highest elected office in the National Church of Scotland. In 1967 he was appointed to the House of Lords. And, after many years of relentlessly calling upon the National Church to take a stand on unilateral nuclear disarmament, MacLeod lived to witness the Church of Scotland's General Assembly call on the British government to dismantle its weapons of mass destruction.

In his last days in Edinburgh, as people visited him at his family home on Learmonth Terrace, MacLeod would often quote the

Beatitudes of Jesus, especially "Blessed are the peacemakers for they will be called children of God" (Matthew 5:9). He never abandoned his passion for peace. When someone asked him how he had remained so steadfast in his position, he humorously replied, "I have remained single-minded on these matters over the years by being stone deaf."

Not long before he died, MacLeod was sharing lunch one day with his son Maxwell and the leader of the Iona community, Ron Ferguson. After lunch Max and Ron stepped out to pick up a newspaper at a local shop. When they were out, MacLeod fell over. He had not seriously hurt himself, but he could not get up. Always something of a joker, MacLeod decided that when Max and Ron returned he would keep his eyes closed to give them a fright. His son rushed to his side and knelt down. At which point MacLeod opened one eye and said to him, "Do you believe in nonviolence?" Now Max had never totally agreed with his father on the principle of nonviolence, but thinking this might be the last time MacLeod would ask the question, he said, "Okay, father. Okay. I believe in nonviolence." To which MacLeod responded, looking at Ron Ferguson, "Take note of the time and the place at which this man said he believed in nonviolence." Forever a campaigner!

George MacLeod died in Edinburgh on August 27, 1991. At that point I was still leading the Abbey community on Iona. We knew there would be public services and memorials in the weeks and months ahead to mark the life and vision of MacLeod, so on that summer day on Iona we decided simply to gather in the Abbey church in silent thanksgiving and to read aloud some of MacLeod's prayers. The church was filled with guests and residents of the Abbey, islanders from their homes and crofts, and day visitors from all over the world. This is one of the prayers I read that day:

> Be Thou, triune God, in the midst of us as we give thanks for those who have gone from the sight of earthly eyes. They, in Thy nearer presence, still worship with us in the mystery of the one family in heaven and on earth....

If it be Thy holy will, tell them how we love them, and how we miss them, and how we long for the day when we shall meet with them again....

Strengthen us to go on in loving service of all Thy children. Thus shall we have communion with Thee and, in Thee, with our beloved ones. Thus shall we come to know, within ourselves, that there is no death and that only a veil divides, thin as gossamer.[26]

We loved MacLeod and we love his memory. In part, this is because he was so faithful to the vision of nonviolence. He prophetically showed us one of the features of the rebirthing of God from deep within the human soul. It was not just a *vision* that he shared with us. It was a *commitment* to embodying that vision in the relationships of our lives and our world. As he said to me on that first occasion of our meeting years ago, "Newell, what are we going to do about this?" That question still resonates. It still vibrates through the thin veil that separates us from MacLeod and other great prophets of peace who have gone before us. With one another and with their inspiration we pray, "Strengthen us to go on in loving service of all Thy children."

Chapter 7

Reconnecting with the Unconscious

Eco-theologian Thomas Berry says the universe is so amazing in its interrelatedness that it must have been dreamt into being. He also says our situation today as an earth community is so desperate—we are so far from knowing how to save ourselves from the ecological degradations we are part of—that we must dream the way forward. We must summon, from the unconscious, ways of seeing that we know nothing of yet, visions that emerge from deeper within us than our conscious rational minds.

Similarly the rebirthing of our true depths will involve a reconnection with the unconscious. It will demand a fresh releasing within us of the world of dreams, myths, and the imagination. Whether as individuals or collectively as nations and religious traditions, new beginnings will be born among us when we open to the well of what we do not yet know or what we have forgotten deep within.

Opening to the Well of the Imagination

On Iona there is a wellspring on the northern side of Dun I. It is called the Well of Eternal Youth. It has pre-Christian significance and is associated

with St. Brigid of Kildare, the fifth-century Irish saint who is much celebrated in the Western isles of Scotland—or the Hebrides as they are
also known, meaning the islands of Bride or Brigid. Legend has it that her
mother was a Christian and her stepfather a Druid priest. She combines
within herself the stream of Christian devotion in confluence with the
wisdom of pre-Christian religious insight. So she is often associated with
sites in the Celtic world, like the Well of Eternal Youth on Iona, that were
considered sacred long before the advent of Christianity.

Brigid of Kildare is the saint who straddles the Christian and the
pre-Christian. Even the name of her monastic community in Ireland,
Kildare, simply means the Church of the Oaks. It was a holy oak grove
from Druidic times that was baptized by Brigid into Celtic Christian
practice. She embodied a devotion to Christ and an honoring of pre-
Christian wisdom, especially its reverencing of nature and the healing
properties of the earth.

According to legend, Brigid was the midwife and wet nurse of the
Christ Child. She is described as the barmaid at the inn in Bethlehem
where Mary and Joseph seek shelter. There is no room at the inn but
Brigid provides them with space in the stable. At the moment of the
birth, Brigid midwives the Christ Child and then suckles him at her
breast. It is a story that points to the way in which the Christian Gospel
in the Celtic world was nurtured on the nature mysticism that preceded
Christianity. The myths and legends of that world were incorporated
into its celebration of Christ. They were like an old testament to the
new revelation. There was no concern about historical discontinuity.
The anachronism of a fifth-century Irish saint being present at a first-
century Middle Eastern birth did not worry the Celts. This was a story
that allowed two worlds to become one.

On the island of Iona it was said that Brigid would appear at the
Well of Eternal Youth on the summer solstice when, in the Western
isles of Scotland, darkness does not fully come until after midnight.
So, even well into the nineteenth century, people would gather in the
late twilight of midsummer's night to seek Brigid's blessing. Not surprisingly, Brigid's blessing was sought in the twilight, for she belongs to the
liminal realm between worlds that is represented by the fading of light

and the approaching darkness. It is the time ruled neither by the sun nor by the moon but by the meeting of the two. It is the time of the two lights, twilight.

Into this liminal realm, between the known and the unknown, we are invited to enter if we are to learn more of the way forward in our lives as individuals and as communities and nations. This is why, in so much Celtic storytelling and legend, lovers meet and worlds conjoin in the twilight. It is the coming together of the masculine and the feminine. It is the convergence of the unseen world of those who have gone before us and this present dimension of space and time in which the seen and the physical dominate. It may be a time of encountering messengers from the invisible realms of the universe that are linked inextricably to our realm, but at the same time transcend us in our struggle with unknown forces of darkness within and without. This is also why, in so much Eastern spiritual practice, the early hours of dawn are viewed as the time of meditation, when night and day are commingling in ways that more readily allow us to move from the known to the unknown and from the nameable to the ineffable. This is why I sought the predawn hours of early morning in which to begin the writing of this book each day. This is the time that is closer to dream life and the half-wakeful state of knowing in which both light and shadow come forth and all things appear as one.

The Marriage of the Conscious and the Unconscious

Perhaps the greatest modern prophet of the unconscious was Carl Jung (1875–1961), the founder of analytical psychology. He devoted his life to accessing the psyche, a word that derives from the Greek *psukh*, meaning "breath" or "soul." Jung believed that wholeness was to be found by coming back into relationship with the unconscious depths of the soul. We long for what is beneath the surface. "The treasure," he says, "lies in the depths of the water."[1] We long for what we do not yet know to emerge from hidden and unawakened depths within us into the light of day, into the realm of full consciousness. The way to access these depths is through the world of dreams, intuition, and imagination.

When Jung speaks of our *consciousness*, he is referring to what we already know, to what we are aware or fully conscious of. By the *unconscious*, on the other hand, he is referring to what we do not yet know or what we have forgotten. He is pointing to that vast realm of unknowing, to the worlds upon worlds within us that have yet to emerge into the light of awareness. Jung distinguishes between what he calls the *personal unconscious* and the *collective unconscious*. The personal unconscious consists of what we have known or experienced individually in the past but which has slipped from consciousness into forgetfulness. The collective unconscious is like a river of images, or archetypes as he calls them, which flow deep within the human soul. They are ours by birthright, a common inheritance, not based on individual experience or knowledge but universally present within us all. It is from this river of the collective unconscious that dreams, myths, and the imagination flow. This is the foundation, says Jung, of what the ancients called the "symphony of all things."[2] It is the one world, the *unus mundus*, from which everything has emerged and to which we must reconnect if we are to be whole again.

Jung says that wholeness consists of bringing together what has been torn apart, whether that be the conscious and the unconscious, the night and the day, the feminine and the masculine, the head and the heart, spirit and matter, the East and the West, the wisdom of one people and that of another, or the life of the human species and the life of every other species on earth. We live, says Jung, in a "painful fragmentariness."[3] We live in a division of the parts. We have separated what God has joined together, the oneness of the universe.

Jung sees the entire world as an unfolding of God. It is a manifesting of the One. A primary feature of this manifestation is that the universe unfolds through "paired opposites."[4] There is the sun and the moon, the feminine and the masculine, the east and the west. There is hot and cold, dry and moist, black and white. Nothing exists without its opposite. Everything has its complementarity. Life wants all days to be followed by nights, the emergence of seed-force in the spring to be balanced by seeds falling back into the ground in autumn. Yet despite the universe's equilibrium, we often live in captivity to the opposites.

We live in the day and know little of the night. We are dominated by masculine energies and suppress our feminine instincts. We are Christians and neglect the wisdom of other traditions. We use our minds and desert our intuition. The list goes on and on and on, the painful fragmentariness of our lives.

Jung distinguishes between what he calls moonlike consciousness and sunlike consciousness.[5] Think of what it is like looking at the world under the full white radiance of the moon. Certainly when I walk under the moon's light at night I am almost speechless. I am filled with wonder because what the moon's light enables me to remember is the oneness of everything I am in the midst of. The hard edges of day are softened by the moon's gentle light, and I see the relationship of all things. When I walk under the sun's light, on the other hand, I am much more ready to speak analytically, noting the uniqueness of the parts and the differentiations among everything around me.

> We long for what we do not yet know to emerge from hidden and unawakened depths within us into the realm of full consciousness. The way to access these depths is through the world of dreams, intuition, and imagination.

Jung's point is that we need both ways of seeing. We need moonlike consciousness and sunlike consciousness. But so much of our culture, including much of our Western Christian inheritance, has been dominated by sunlike consciousness. We have been strong at seeing the uniquenesses and accentuating individuality, but we have forgotten the oneness from which we have come. We have been blind to the *unus mundus* that is deeper than the world of differentiation.

The Hebrew Scriptures offer us visions of the marriage of opposites. "The wolf shall live with the lamb," says the prophet Isaiah, "and the leopard shall lie down with the kid" (Isaiah 11:6). Similarly the Christian Scriptures say that in the kingdom of God people will gather "from east and west" to sit together (Matthew 8:11). These are visions of peace, of a wholeness in which what has been torn apart will be brought back together again.

Jung says that the Spirit is a *coniunctio oppositorum*, a conjoining or bringing together of what is considered opposite—spirit and matter, the night and the day, the one and the many.[6] The Spirit leads to communion, a word that is derived from the Latin *communis*, meaning "one with." To be born of the Spirit is to remember our oneness with each other, with the earth, and with those who seem most different—most threateningly different—from us.

> By listening to our dreams of the night, or the daydreams and intuitions of our wakeful hours, we can access ways of seeing that will truly serve the holy work of bringing back into communion again what has been torn apart in our lives and our world.

Many years ago I had a dream in which I was presiding at communion in Edinburgh's St. Giles Cathedral. The bread and wine were already on the altar. The prayers had been said and I was about to share the gifts with the people. But standing at opposite corners of the altar were two groups. One consisted of members of Amnesty International, passionate about their work for human rights. The other was made up of singers, chanting the most beautiful Gregorian plainsong. Members of each group were holding one of the corners of the altar cloth and they were pulling in opposite directions. The tension was so great that it seemed as if the chalice were going to topple over. I could not continue with the celebration of communion.

The dream speaks of the need to reconcile apparent opposites, in this case the tension between action and contemplation, before we can experience oneness. It also speaks of the desire, from seemingly irreconcilable corners, to have a piece of the altar cloth. The activists were working for justice in their commitment to human rights. The singers were intoning an ancient harmony of the interrelationship of all things. Both longed for oneness. The way forward in our lives is to somehow place ourselves in the middle of such tension, where the wine of the chalice is most disturbed, and allow ourselves to see and affirm the desires for oneness that emerge from both corners. From that central point we must allow ourselves to imagine ways of bringing back into harmony the so-called opposites. The chalice also represents cost and sacrifice. New birth does not occur without pain. It comes with the travail of labor.

Jung says that in the unconscious the opposites lie side by side.[7] It is only up in the conscious world that there is separation. Messages from the unconscious, such as the dream of the altar cloth at St. Giles, are inviting us back into oneness and an awareness that it will be a costly journey. By listening to our dreams of the night, or the daydreams and intuitions of our wakeful hours, we can access ways of seeing that will truly serve the holy work of bringing back into communion again what has been torn apart in our lives and our world. Everything has emerged from the *unus mundus*. By accessing that world, we will find the relationships that are deeper than our differences.

The Promise of Union

George McDonald (1824–1905) was a Scottish novelist who drew heavily on the world of the imagination. He could be described as the J. K. Rowling of the nineteenth century. His works, and especially his fairy tales, were immensely popular. One of his writings, *The Day Boy and the Night Girl*, explores the theme of bringing back into relationship what has been tragically separated. In this case it is the relationship between what Jung calls the "supreme pair of opposites," the relationship between the feminine and the masculine.[8]

McDonald's fairy tale begins with a witch who is wicked because she has a ravenous wolf living in her heart. The wolf's desire, which often controls her, is to rip apart what belongs together. The witch has already ripped open the heart of a royal family. She stole at birth the firstborn child of the princess Aurora, giving the mother the impression that her newborn son had died. She did the same to a family of humble origin, stealing at birth their firstborn child, in this case a daughter.

The little prince and the little girl are kept in separate parts of the witch's castle. They grow up knowing nothing of each other. The prince is forced to be wakeful only during the day. He lives without knowledge of the night and the soft whiteness of the moon's radiance. The girl is allowed only to experience the night. Never has she experienced the direct force of the sun's brightness. The prince, whose hair is wavy and golden like the sun, spends his days riding horses and bravely hunting the creatures of the wood. The girl, on the other hand, has straight, black hair like the night. Never has she been taught to read and reason, as the prince has. Rather, she has been trained only in music and spends her nights freely roaming the woods in relationship with the wild creatures that the prince hunts by day.

The turning point in the tale comes when the prince is pursuing a lion at sunset. Instead of turning back to the castle, as the witch had trained him to do, he follows the lion into the woods and night falls. In the blackness of night the normally brave prince becomes terrified. Driven mad with fear, he flees back to the castle and collapses in the garden. There the girl finds him, prone and shaking with fright. She kneels beside him, gently stroking his face and placing her lips to his forehead. She is in awe of this creature she has never seen before, a man. At first the prince is frightened of her. But, as he lies powerless in the garden by night, his head held in her arms, he begins to be moved by what he has never known before, the presence of a beautiful young woman.

Together they realize they have been living half-lives and that the witch has been holding them in cruel imprisonment. Together they plot their escape. The girl will lead them in the dark intimacy of the night that the prince is so terrified of. The prince will guide them in the glaring brightness of the day that so blinds the unaccustomed eyes of the girl. So by night and by day the prince and the girl make their journey into freedom together.

When the witch discovers they have fled, she is furious. The wolf in her heart so consumes her that she becomes the wolf and sets off at high speed to tear them apart. They see the angry wolf approaching and, not knowing that it is the witch, the prince pulls out his bow and arrow and with one shot fells the wolf with an arrow straight to the heart. It is only when he takes out his sword to cut off the ravenous creature's head that he realizes it is the witch. They are free. The king of the land, on learning their story, grants them the witch's castle as their home. There they are married and eventually give birth to a child. She has blue eyes like her father and black hair like her mother. The prince comes to love the night even more than the day because it is his wife's true home. She comes to love the day even more than the night because it is the prince's true home.

This is a story of the marriage of opposites and of how we live our lives in "painful fragmentariness," in tragic imprisonments that separate us from our authentic self and prevent us from achieving true well-being. It is a story, too, that invites us to be aware of the shadow that lives in our heart, that side of us that can become demented and choose to tear apart rather than hold together. But if Jung had written this fairy tale, I do not believe he would have killed off the witch. He would have looked for some way of reintegrating her, of bringing the shadow back into relationship with the light. For the reality is that we cannot simply kill off the witch. The shadow is alive and will always be with us. The challenge in our lives and our world is to imagine a way forward that fully recognizes the presence of the shadow. In every moment, relationship, and new beginning we have the capacity to choose division rather than oneness, separateness rather than relationship. The question is how we will confidently recognize the shadow's presence without giving it room to be destructive.

Jung believes that deep within all opposites is a hidden attraction. He calls this the "promise of union."9 We see it in McDonald's fairy tale, when the prince and the girl first meet. They are so different. The prince has known only the day. He is a creature of sunlike consciousness. The girl, on the other hand, has known only the night and has been shaped by her experience of the moon's light. Yet when they meet, they fall in love with each other, even though the prince is a bit slower to know it because of his fear of the unknown. This hidden attraction is true in relation to the supreme pair of opposites—the masculine and the feminine. But it is also true for every set of opposites. Deeper than the fears that drive us into opposition are hidden attractions waiting to be awakened. Our role is to help uncover and release the promise of union that is in all things.

The unconscious invites us to discover the bliss of oneness. It does not diminish our uniqueness and individuality. Rather, it is a conjoining that delights in our differences and honors them. This is why, in most of the great spiritual traditions of the world, true sexual relationship is regarded as an experience of the Divine because in such engagement we forget our separateness. Our whole being moves as one with the other in an enfolding and intermingling that goes deeper than our differences. True union delights in difference. It does not smother it. This is as true of the universe's oneness as it is in our most intimate relationships of longing. It is the bliss that can inspire us as a whole people as much as it delights us as lovers in union.

> The unconscious invites us to discover the bliss of oneness. It does not diminish our uniqueness and individuality. Rather, it is a conjoining that delights in our differences and honors them.

Jung observes that the marriage of opposites leads to pregnancy. Bringing together those who seem to be opposites produces new birth. This, he says, is where God is "born."[10] This is where what has never been before comes into being. If there is to be a rebirthing of the Sacred within us as nations, as religious traditions, as communities and families, we need to move into relationship with those who are considered unlike us. From this new birth emerges.

The American writer Ken Wilber speaks of a threefold journey toward wholeness.[11] We are born, he says, in a world of undifferentiated oneness. At birth we make no distinction between ourselves and our mothers and everything else around us. It is all one. Then the ego begins to develop. Wilber calls this essential second stage differentiation. We distinguish between ourselves and our environment. Consciousness of the self has been born. But the problem for so many of us in the West, and in so much of our Western culture and religion, is that we get stuck at this second stage. We define ourselves in terms of our separateness, our ego, or the ego of our nation or our religion. We fail to move toward the final stage of wholeness, which Wilber calls "differentiated oneness." This stage fully incorporates the first two, namely the oneness from which we have come and the differentiation of our selfhood. Wholeness consists of remembering and honoring the oneness, while not diminishing the precious uniqueness of our individualities.

What gets in the way of this movement toward wholeness is the ego. This is not to put down the ego. It is our sacred faculty of self-awareness and consciousness and the power to choose freely. But again and again it strives to be the center, rather than serving the Center. It pretends to be the one, instead of being rooted in the One. Jung says that we need to "celebrate a Last Supper" with our ego.[12] We need to die to the way in which our ego claims to be Lord so that we can truly live the dignity of our selfhood in the commonweal of relationship with all things. We need to celebrate this last supper not just once, but again and again and again, in every moment, encounter, and relationship, if we are to be truly free.

Dreaming the Way Forward

How can we serve the oneness that we are part of—not simply as individuals but as nations and as religious traditions? How can the uniqueness of our Christian identity and story serve not simply our own preservation but the well-being of the world? Part of the answer lies in allowing ourselves to dream the Christian story onward, allowing our imagination to draw from the living well of the unconscious within us. Otherwise, our story gets stuck. Our myth freezes into fixed form and we no longer deeply serve the unfolding journey of the universe. As Jung says, "God refuses to abide by traditions, no matter how sacred."[13] Life flows, he says; it doesn't stagnate.[14] We have no claim to endless perpetuity. If the river of our Christian story is not flowing, we will cease to be, for we will cease to be in tune with the very nature of the universe, forever seeking new form, forever unfolding into what has never been known before. Just as in sleep every night we descend into the unconscious to be renewed, so our Christian story needs to reenter the world of dreaming and imagining to be born anew.

The first time I ever worked with my brother Rabbi Nahum Ward-Lev in New Mexico, I was struck by his approach to the Hebrew Scriptures as essentially a story that is living and forever unfolding. On one of the first mornings of our week together, I had been teaching the sacredness of the human soul and contrasting this Celtic emphasis with the Mediterranean focus on sin. There ensued a heated discussion about the doctrine of original sin, which has been used by Western Christianity to give the impression that what is deepest in us is opposed to God instead of being of God. In the afternoon Nahum led us through a study of Torah in which we explored the story of humanity's beginnings in Genesis chapter 1. He introduced the study by saying that Judaism does not have doctrine; it has story. In studying the Torah together we are to ask questions of the story and allow it to speak anew.

> If the river of our Christian story is not flowing, we will cease to be, for we will cease to be in tune with the very nature of the universe, forever seeking new form, forever unfolding into what has never been known before.

What if we had allowed our Christian story to freely live and unfold, rather than trying to nail down its meanings with doctrine? As the Gospel accounts of Jesus say, he taught in story form. "Without a parable," says St. Matthew, "he told them nothing" (Matthew 13:34). Christianity has often avoided the descent back into the unconscious and the world of the unfolding imagination for fear of what may be found there. The yet unknown might challenge us to change. The untamed, imaginal realm within the human soul might call us to do something we have been trained not even to consider.

This is what we see happening in early Christianity when cen-
tralized doctrine has not yet been established to inhibit the free flow
of vision and its unfolding story of Christ. We find Peter, the leader
of the disciples after Jesus's death, falling asleep one day just before
lunch on a rooftop by the seaside in Joppa. He dreams of the heav-
ens opening and something like a large sheet being lowered to the
ground by its four corners. In it are creatures of every description.
He hears a voice telling him to take and eat. But Peter objects on the
grounds of what he had been taught in his religious practice and says,
"By no means, Lord, for I have never eaten anything that is profane
or unclean." And the voice replies, "What God has made clean, you
must not call profane" (Acts 10:14–15). But Peter does not get it, so
the dream needs to come a second time and a third time. Finally, Peter
opens his heart to the vision and allows it to change him. This marks
the beginnings of Christianity moving beyond the tight boundaries
that had separated life into categories of the clean and the unclean or
between one people and the rest of humanity or between one place
and every place. Everything that has emerged from the womb of the
universe is clean. It is of God.

If the Christian story is to live again in ways that will truly bless the
world, we need to access the world of the unconscious, the *unus mundus*,
where we and all things are one. Then we can allow the story of Christ's
birth to be born anew and to point to the birth of every child. Yes, we
will always delight in the particularity of our story, rooted as it is in the
birth of one holy child in Palestine two thousand years ago. But if our
story is living, we will release it in ways that we have not yet imagined
to serve the essential sacredness of every child who is born. As the
Indian Jesuit Antony de Mello says, "Listen to the song the angels sang
the day you were born."[15] That song is sung for every human being and
for every life-form. It is continuous, sung without interruption, as the
universe unfolds into ever-new form. It is sung in the full knowledge of
the mighty forces of wrong that are ready to pounce on the vulnerable
innocence of everything that is born.

Similarly, we need to allow our Christian story of the empty tomb
to be reborn. It will always have its origins in Palestine, soon after the

death of Jesus of Nazareth. We will always retell it in the context of Jesus coming alive again in the hearts and lives of his closest followers, in ways that led to unimagined liberation from fear and unprecedented expressions of compassion. But that story, so cherished in our Christian memory, needs to further unfold in ways we have not yet known, way beyond the bounds of one person or one community at one point in time. As the great prophet of liberation in Central America, Archbishop Oscar Romero, said in the face of the death threats from his country's military junta that finally took his life, "If they kill me I will rise again in the people of El Salvador."[16] Our story can be set free to serve at the suffering of any person and any people as well as at the tender moments of grief that visit each one of us as individuals and families. Nothing can prevent the personal beauty and particular passions that are deep within those whom we have loved, as well as deep within each one of us, from rising again in new form in the unfolding story of the universe. Nothing.

> If the Christian story is to live again in ways that will truly bless the world, we need to access the world of the unconscious, the *unus mundus*, where we and all things are one.

What is said of the stories of the birth and the empty tomb can equally be said of the story of Pentecost, when legend has it that the Spirit in Jesus came alive in the disciples, what Jung calls the "Christification" of the disciples.[17] They are described as speaking a language that could be understood by people of every nation visiting Jerusalem. The same passion that had led Jesus to break through boundaries of separation between the respectable and outcasts, between the religious and the unclean, between one people and another was now filling the disciples.

Perhaps the least preached-upon text in the whole of Christian Scripture is Jesus saying in St. John's Gospel that those who follow him will not only continue his work but do "greater works" than he (John 14:12). Do we believe this? The passion for oneness is so deep in the matter of the universe that it will be reborn, no matter what opposing forces are put in place, and will multiply into greater and greater works of oneness for the healing of the earth. The well from which Jesus drew is living. It is deep within each one of us.

On Iona, when we gather as pilgrims at the Well of Eternal Youth, there is often playfulness around the little pool that is nestled between enormous pieces of granite that look as if they were carelessly tossed there by giants of ancient times. People take turns kneeling by the waters to sip or to bathe their faces or splash others. Together we ask what is trying to rise up from the waters of the human soul today. What are the new dreams, visions, and imaginings? What are the eternal youthfulnesses deep in the collective unconscious that are trying to emerge for our renewal and well-being?

Here we can seek the blessing of St. Brigid, who seems so comfortable in this liminal place between the dark waters of the unconscious and the light of awareness at its surface, between the unknown that is stirring within us and the fresh visions that are trying to emerge. In the Celtic world, Brigid's feast day is the beginning of spring, the first day of February. It is a day of new beginnings as the fertile earth begins to stir into motion again. It is known as *imbolc,* which simply means "in the belly." This is where new life is, in the belly of the earth, in the belly of the human soul. It is not yet seen, but it is stirring. Before long it will try to come forth among us as new birth, with a vulnerability that needs protection and a sacredness that calls for celebration.

As Peter said on the day of Pentecost, when Christianity was born, "Your young shall see visions and your old shall dream dreams" (Acts 2:17). It is a rebirth we are seeking, not just a resuscitation. It is a fresh springing forth from the unknown depths of the human soul. New vision, new dreams, a new Pentecost, a rebirthing of Christ in us. Shall we open to it?

Chapter 8

Reconnecting
with Love

Perhaps the most obvious feature of a rebirthing of God in our lives and our world is at the same time its most undefinable feature—love.

As an old man, looking back over his long lifetime of serving human consciousness and trying to bring into awareness and expression the unknown depths of the soul, Carl Jung said of the mystery of love, "I have never been able to explain what it is."[1] He acknowledged that St. Paul comes close when, in his great hymn to love, he writes that love "bears all things" and "endures all things" (1 Corinthians 13:7). "These words say all there is to be said," wrote Jung. "Nothing can be added to these."[2] But in the end Jung feels that the best way to express the ineffability of love is to "name the unknown by the more unknown ... that is, by the name of God."[3]

God Is Love

Perhaps this is what John the Beloved was trying to do when he said "God is love" (1 John 4:16). This briefest description of love is probably also its profoundest. It is attempting to say the unsayable, endeavoring to express what is beyond definition by employing the even more inexplicable word *God*. It is making the boldest of claims, that God is love and love is God. "Those who abide in love abide in God," as St. John goes on to say (1 John 4:16). The rebirthing of love in our lives is the sine qua non of the rebirthing of God. Without it, says St. Paul, we are like "a noisy gong or a clanging cymbal" (1 Corinthians 13:1). Without it we are nothing.

On the isle of Iona there is a sixteen-foot-high stone-carved cross from the tenth century called St. Martin's Cross. It stands in front of the Abbey. In Christianity the cross historically has been our most prominent symbol. The word *symbol* is derived from the Greek *sumbolon*, meaning "to throw together." A symbol is a throwing together of the known and the unknown, of what can be expressed with what is inexpressible. In this case it is taking what we know, a cross, and throwing it together with what is beyond definition, love. In Christianity the cross becomes a symbol of God's love, a symbol of the inexplicable. Because we are made of God, it also becomes a symbol of what is unutterable or indefinable in us, our longing for love and our capacity in love to endure all things.

Jung says that the cross is the Christian totality symbol.[4] Essentially it is a mandala, an ancient representation of wholeness, or the totality of all things. Say we draw a circle around it, as the community of John the Beloved did in Asia Minor in its early cross design with equidistant vertical and horizontal lines touching the surrounding circle. The Celtic tradition later did the same thing by placing a circle superimposed over the heart of the cross. With this added design element, the cross's mandala feature becomes apparent. It has four quadrants and four primary points. We see north and south, east and west. We see the above and the below, the left and the right. In the cross these opposites are joined. It is a way of saying that heaven and earth, East and West, the Divine and the human, the life of one nation and the life of its polar opposite, can be brought together. The place where the lines intersect is at the heart of the cross. The only force that has the power to truly bring together the apparent opposites in our lives and our world is love.

In my travels I meet many people on both sides of the Atlantic who belong to the Christian household, either by birth or by intentional practice, who find it impossible to identify with, or in many cases even to tolerate, the use of this most enduring Christian symbol. This is usually because, in their experience, the cross has been so strongly linked with a particular doctrine of salvation. They have either been explicitly taught or given the impression that a price needed to be paid for God's forgiveness, and that price was the death of Jesus. The teaching is often referred to as the doctrine of substitutionary atonement. Although a payment needed to be made, says the doctrine, we are not worthy to make payment ourselves, so a substitute sacrifice was needed. Jesus died on our behalf to propitiate the anger of God.

One of the problems with this doctrine is that it runs counter to our deepest experiences of love. Who are the people who have most loved us in our lives amid our failures and betrayals? Could we imagine them ever requiring payment to forgive us? True love is free. Perhaps so much wrong has been done by this doctrine that the cross has become an irredeemable symbol for many, both within the Christian household and beyond. But I hope not. I hope it can be redeemed because, essentially, it is a symbol of the mystery at the heart of Christianity's great gift to the world—the belief that love can reconcile all things.

The cross points to the love that so endured in Jesus for the poorest and most powerless of his people that he found the strength to go to Jerusalem to confront the holders of false power in his nation. It points to the love that so lived in Gandhi and Archbishop Oscar Romero, in civil rights activist Rosa Parks (1913–2005), and in countless others who, knowing the likely cost of their passion for justice—the threat of imprisonment or death—nevertheless continued on their chosen pathway. It is a love that we have experienced in those who have been most faithful to us in our families and friendships and that we most

> Who are the people who have most loved us in our lives amid our failures and betrayals? Could we imagine them ever requiring payment to forgive us? True love is free.

long for in the midst of brokenness and fragmentation in our lives and our world.

During the writing of this chapter I attended the funeral of a young woman named Mandy whom I first met years ago when she was still a teenager living in one of the poorest areas of Edinburgh. In some ways, even though she was exceedingly attractive, bright, and gifted, her life was a continuous series of brokenness and fragmentation. She grew up in an orphanage, followed by a trail of foster homes and institutions in which she experienced the neglect and abuse that so often characterize such journeys. She was pregnant by the age of sixteen. Then there were years of drug abuse, constant moves from house to house, ill health, the amputation of a leg, and then finally the heart attack that took her life. But the song that was sung at her funeral, and a song that I can still hear her warmly singing as a teenager, expressed her deep longing:

> Bind us together, Lord,
> Bind us together
> With cords that cannot be broken.
> Bind us together, Lord,
> Bind us together,
> Bind us together with love.[5]

Amid the painful fragmentariness of her life, she longed for the strands of her relationships to be woven together. It was a longing for the love that can endure all things, that is stronger than any broken-ness or fragmentation. Speaking to her son and daughter after the funeral, it was clear to me that, despite the tragic list of brokenness upon brokenness in her life and in her mothering, love's seed, sown in them by Mandy, was alive and would not be undone: "cords that cannot be broken."

This longing that is so deep in the human soul is also deep in the very matter of the universe. It is the yearning at the heart of everything, to move in relationship. That is why the Celtic high-standing cross, rooted firmly in the earth and standing tall in the great cathedral of nature, beckons us to join the yearning that is in all things. "We know," says St. Paul, "that the whole creation has been groaning in labor pains until now" (Romans 8:22). Our yearning is part of a cosmic yearning, to live in oneness.

One of the distinct features of the Celtic cross is its conjoining of symbols. There is the cross symbol—pointing to the way of Christ, to the love that can bear all things—and there is the circle symbol— pointing to the oneness or interrelatedness of all things. One of the significant features of the Celtic cross is that the cross symbol and the circle symbol share the same center. They emerge from the same point. So the Celtic cross celebrates that Christ and creation spring forth from the same Source. They both emerge from the heart of God. The deeper we move in the Christ mystery, the closer we come to the One who is the origin of creation. The deeper we move in the mystery of Creation, the closer we come to the Presence that Christ embodies. Deepest in both, and deepest in us, is the yearning for union, to remember the oneness from which we have come, and to live and move as one again.

Saying Yes to the Heart of the Other

One of the great prophets of love in the modern world was Simone Weil (1909–1943), described by her contemporary, the existential novelist Albert Camus (1913–1960), as "the only great spirit of our times."[6] She was a philosopher, a mystic, and a political activist. As a French Jew, she saw the Nazi occupation of her homeland, fleeing Paris on June 13, 1940, only hours before German forces laid siege to the capital. Eventually, she set sail from the south of France to find exile in the United States and then in Britain.

Weil believed that the universe is essentially a vibration of God.[7] Drawing on her Jewish inheritance, she saw everything as spoken into being by God. At the heart of that divine utterance is the sound or vibration of love. The universe is an expression of love and everything in the universe is essentially a means to love.[8] The rising sun is a means to love, as is the whiteness of the moon at night. Every life-form, the shape of the weeping willow by the distant pond, the song of the robin in the hedgerow, the light in the eyes of every creature—all these are means to love. I am a means to love, as are you, your children, and your nation. Do we know that? Do we know that this is our sacred role in the world?

When we become aware that what is deepest in the heart of the other is a resonance, or living vibration, of the Sacred—whether that be in a tree or another plant, a wild creature, or another human being—we find ourselves wanting to say yes. We find that our heart is drawn toward the heart of the other. If we stay focused on the sacred center of the other, says Weil, we will be drawn into what she calls our "nuptial yes" to God, the desire to live in union and to marry what is deepest in us to what is deepest in the other.[9] "We are created for this consent," she says, "and for this alone."[10]

This "nuptial yes" has the power to change our lives. We no longer confine the other into the fixed categories of race or gender, creed or sexual orientation. The other is set free to be a unique and living expression of the One, no longer bound by the predetermined definitions of outward classification. We not only reverence the true heart of the other but also bring the vibration of our own being into harmony with the sacred sound of theirs.

> The deeper we move in the mystery of Creation, the closer we come to the Presence that Christ embodies. Deepest in us is the yearning for union, to remember the oneness from which we have come, and to live and move as one again.

When I was a student of theology in Scotland, Jack, one of my best boyhood friends from Canada, went through a sexual orientation crisis. He experienced a nervous breakdown. Nearly everything in his culture, his religious upbringing, and his immediate family context opposed the realization that was stirring in him—that he was gay. I was not there to be supportive at the time. But he came through the crisis, clear and strong in his identity. When Ali and I moved back to Canada in the early 1980s, Jack came to see us and to share his story.

I was eager to show him my support, even though part of me felt uncomfortable about his sexuality. In my theological training in

Edinburgh, I had intellectually worked through the idea of homosexuality, but that was simply working through an idea. Here, on the other hand, was one of my best boyhood friends, and he was gay, and I was experiencing another response in my gut. But Ali and I were clear in our intention. We wanted to extend a hand of love to him. So we invited Jack and his partner for a meal.

A few days before the dinner, Jack called to say that he and Peter were vegetarian. Now this was the early 1980s and vegetarianism was as strange to me then as homosexuality. But we dutifully prepared the meal. When they arrived, we were all very polite, everyone trying to get it just right. Then, as Ali brought in the main course, placing it on the dining room table, she said, "It's been a long time since I've made a homosexual meal." There was stunned silence and then we all collapsed into laughter together, tears streaming down our faces. From then on, I was just fine. No more gut reactions. Ali's slip had expressed the unspoken discomfort all of us were feeling, and that was all we needed. We were free now to remember the essence of Jack and Peter and to forget the label of their sexual orientation.

When we say yes to the true heart of one another, we move back into relationship. This is what the Dalai Lama calls the kinship of all being and what Weil refers to as the new saintliness.[11] It is not like the old notion of saintliness that has so dominated much of our religious inheritance, in which we have been given the impression that holiness is about looking away from this world to a spiritual home that is above or beyond us. For Weil the universe, here and now, is our true home. We have no other country, she says.[12] This is where the Sacred is to be found, in the body of the earth, in our human bodies, and in the body of our communities and nations.

This is not to romanticize the universe and the many bodies of which it consists, our beautiful and broken bodies, the glorious and infected bodies of earth's creatures, and the mysterious and challenging interrelationship of all things. Everything, says Weil, can offer "resistance to love."[13] What we know in our families and in the most intimate relationships of our lives is that we have the capacity to choose not to love. This capacity, with its wide range of expressions, can be found in all things. There is a preference for oneness in the universe, from the atomic level upward, but it is not predetermined or fixed. Everything can, at some level, choose to violate the harmony. Everything has the capacity to resist oneness.

> Everything can, at some level, choose to violate the harmony. Everything has the capacity to resist oneness.

This is our home—the universe—where our love, our capacity to say yes, is to be focused. It is too easy, says Weil, to love an imaginary home, a spiritual country, or an unseen dimension somewhere beyond us or other than us, because we can turn it into anything we wish.[14] "Love needs reality," she says.[15] Or, as we have already heard St. John say, "You cannot hate your brother or sister and love God" (1 John 4:20; adapted). You cannot do it because they are one. Similarly, you cannot turn your gaze from the universe and claim to be looking for God. For God is here and now, inseparably woven into the fabric of our being and into the very matter of the universe.

Giving Up Our Imaginary Position as the Center

Perhaps the most significant turning point in Simone Weil's life came in the spring of 1937, when she was touring Assisi in Italy. She visited the Church of St. Mary of the Angels, which contains the Portiuncula, the chapel that St. Francis in the twelfth century was instructed in a vision to rebuild. It became for him a powerful symbol of the urgent need to rebuild Christianity. In this church in Assisi Weil first experienced the Sacred Presence. "I was compelled," she writes, "for the first time in my life to go down on my knees."[16]

This marked the beginning of a conscious spiritual journey in Weil's life and led eventually to her daily discipline of prayer, which she called "absolutely unmixed attention."[17] It is an "attention which is so full," she said, "that the 'I' disappears."[18] Meditative prayer was a time to bring her full awareness to the heart of life in a way that further trained her to be attentive to the heart of every moment. Although she was Jewish by birth, the prayer she chose to use on a daily basis was the Lord's Prayer, attributed to Jesus. This did not mean she felt the need to become a Christian. In fact, as she later writes, "I have never once had, even for a moment, the feeling that God wants me to be in the Church."[19] There is so much to love in the world that is way beyond the Church, she said. "The real presence of God is the beauty of the universe."[20] The Real Presence is not confined to one particular religious tradition or one particular practice or sacramental action. It is present everywhere and it is everywhere that we are to bow to the Presence with total attention.

Weil's feeling compelled to kneel is at the heart of her vision and practice. It is not just a perception of Presence. It is a response to Presence. It is not just believing in God, but also embodying belief, translating perception into physical action, kneeling. It is an act that can reconnect us to what is deepest within us and what is deepest within one another and all things.

Why do we not more often kneel, both literally and in our hearts? This is not about putting ourselves down, and it is certainly not about bending to the ego of another or to the ego of systemic power, whether that be the male domination that has undergirded our culture or the consumerism that drives our lifestyle. Rather, it is about emptying ourselves of our false divinity, says Weil, so that our true divinity may rise.[21] It is about giving up our imaginary position as the center of the universe and finding that the true center is everywhere.[22] It is about dying to the way in which our ego, both individual and collective, tries stubbornly to be in charge, rather than faithfully letting go to the Self who is within all selves.

> Why do we not more often kneel, both literally and in our hearts? It is about emptying ourselves of our false divinity so that our true divinity may rise.

One of the things I so admire about the Islamic tradition is the Muslim practice of kneeling, and not simply kneeling but placing the whole body facedown on the ground. Regardless of where they are—I've observed this Islamic practice in airports and other public places of transportation—Muslims simply roll out their prayer mats and kneel, each one of them touching their head and then their whole body to the ground in prayer. Prayer is not simply bringing our mind or heart into relationship with the Sacred, but bringing our whole being into contact with the Holy, including our mind, heart, body, and the deepest physical and sexual energies of our being. It is a reconnecting of everything that is within us.

One of the first times that Ali and I shared a meal with a Muslim family, we were only halfway through the evening meal when they explained they would have to leave us for a while. The sun was about to set and I realized they wanted to pray at the approach of nightfall, which is Islamic custom. I asked if we might join them. I shall always remember how their faces lit up. They looked so delightedly surprised. Why would Christians want to join the prayer of Muslims? Why would these Christians want to get down on the floor and offer their whole being in prayer? It is so sad to think of how we are perceived by others. The sadness relates primarily to how justified other traditions are in assuming that most of us are not serious about prayer, that we do not feel compelled, as Weil did, to go down on our knees, not only daily but many times daily.

> Weil says to be made of love is to remember that we are made of desire. We are made of holy longing.

Weil says that in prayer we remember we are made of God and thus made of love. To be made of love, she says, is to remember that we are made of desire.[23] We are made of holy longing. Weil tells the Native American story of the origins of light. In the eternal darkness at the beginning of time, says the legend, a raven, unable to find food, longed for light. Out of that longing for light the earth was illumined.

Weil calls this the "efficacy of desire."[24] We not only long for what is, but also for what is yet to be. Our longing for what is yet to be is part of the birth of what is yet to come. To long for love in our lives and our world is to be part of the creation of love. To desire wellness for our families and the earth is to stir energies deep within us that can be transfigured into words and actions of well-being for the world. Perhaps it is God's desire for oneness that keeps the universe moving in relationship. This is the holy desire that we can be part of, to long for oneness even in the most broken and apparently God-forsaken places of our lives and our world. Desire leads to conception and conception leads to birth. This is the efficacy of desire.

There Is No Distinction between Love and Justice

In May 1942 Weil sailed to the United States. But within months she returned to Europe, to the United Kingdom, so that she could be closer to her homeland. There she joined the provisional French government and offered her skills as a writer to the French Resistance movement. "The Gospel makes no distinction between the love of our neighbor and justice," she said.[25] To love others is to come close to them, to identify with them, and to do all in our power to shelter them and work for their well-being. This is what she knew she must do for her suffering brothers and sisters in France.

To truly love, she believed, is to know how to say no to the false use of power. It is to learn how to denounce the abuse of force, to avoid being enthralled by it, neither to fear it nor to pursue it.[26] It is to practice detachment from power, not in terms of being naive to its uses or unengaged in its workings but in terms of not worshipping it, not adulating it. This is the detachment that we see in Jesus's refusal to be intimidated by the power of Pontius Pilate, the Roman governor of Judaea. At Jesus's trial, when Pilate asks him, "Do you not know that I have power to release you, and power to crucify you?" Jesus responds, "You would have no power over me unless it had been given you from above" (John 19:10–11). This is to refuse to deify power.

To truly love is to work for a just equity of power between nations, races, and genders, and in our day-to-day relationships and transactions. It is to oppose all patterns of power over another. This is why Weil appeals again and again to the ancient symbol of the scales of justice, which represent a balance between one and the other. In the scales that Lady Justice holds, if there is inequity the scales tip in one direction or the other. This is as true in our most intimate relationships as it is in the great affairs of nations. Love is never about one partner dominating the other. True justice is never about coercing the other. It is only truly attained when the two are able to say yes to each other and to conjoin in ways that honor each other. That, says Weil, is why true love and true justice require consent.[27] They do not ignore the free choice of the other. Which is why it is as impossible for one nation to impose true justice on another, or for one people to dictate what is best for another people, as it is for a lover to claim true bliss if sexual union has been forced on another. Mutuality of consent is the very essence of justice. It is at the heart of love.

When we pray for the world using the prayer that Jesus taught his disciples, as Weil the Jew did, and when we pray by revering the cross as a symbol of the love that can bear all things, as Weil also did, we are praying for a true and just balance between ourselves in the world, as individuals, nations, races, and species. Weil believed that the cross was a revelation of our capacity for love. The cross of Jesus shows us what we are capable of, that we can love even those who are most opposed to us. This is not our ego's capacity. It is our soul's capacity. This is not the strength of the small self. It is the strength of the Great Self at the very heart of our being, the Self into whose depths we can let go to find the strength that will bear all things.

As Christians, we have much to learn from Weil and from the many men and women well beyond the bounds of our Christian household who revere the wisdom and the way of Jesus. As Martin Buber (1868–1965), the great Jewish philosopher, said, "I do not believe *in* Jesus but I do believe *with* him."[28] What if Christianity had gotten that one right? What if we had realized long ago that the important thing is not getting the world to believe what we believe, getting others to subscribe to particular beliefs about Jesus? The important thing is inviting the world to believe *with* Jesus, to believe in the way of love.

A number of years ago I was invited to give some talks at the Episcopal Cathedral in St. Petersburg, Florida. A dear musician friend of mine, Fran McKendree, was also invited to be part of the program.

The coordinator asked us well in advance if we would be willing one evening to take the event into the city, rather than everything happening within the walls of the cathedral. She also suggested and arranged that this could happen at the Atlanta Bread Company, a coffee shop and bakery in downtown St. Petersburg. Fran and I both agreed that this was a great idea. We then proceeded to forget about the great idea until the fated day arrived.

Fran and I got together that morning to talk about what we were going to do in the evening at the Atlanta Bread Company. The more we talked about it, the more we realized, "Yes, what on earth *are* we going to do?" The thought of trying to teach and sing in a public place like a busy downtown coffee shop filled us with terror. We considered heading immediately for the airport, but decided that would be cowardly.

In the end we agreed that I should tell the biblical story of the human journey and that Fran would weave in songs here and there. So I began with the Genesis account of the conception of earth and the emergence of humanity. When I got to the era of prophets railing against the injustices of nations, Fran sang Pete Seeger's "Turn, Turn, Turn."

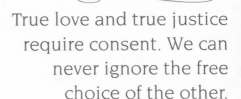

True love and true justice require consent. We can never ignore the free choice of the other.

Then when I told the story of the Annunciation and the angel's promise to Mary of the Christ Child's birth, Fran led us all in singing John Lennon and Paul McCartney's "Let It Be." By now the café was rocking. There were at least fifty people from the cathedral who had come, so we had a strong core. These were now joined by others, visitors to the Atlanta Bread Company, some looking pretty perplexed, getting their coffee and doughnut and leaving very quickly, and others joining to listen and even to sing.

We ended the evening with what I called the Letters of Love, in which I quoted St. Paul's great hymn to love, the love that endures all things. Then Fran played, with everyone standing and some people singing and even dancing, "All You Need Is Love" by Lennon and McCartney. The evening was a bit weighted to the Beatles, and revealed the generation that Fran and I belong to, but we were glad we had not fled to the airport that morning.

I suppose some of the people who were there that evening would have agreed with Martin Buber when he said, "I do not believe *in* Jesus but I do believe *with* him." I suppose good numbers of them would not have called themselves Christian. But that is not what matters. What matters is whether they believe in love. What matters is whether, *with* Jesus, we are following the way of love, for this is all we need. Love is all we need.

To choose love is not something we do once. It is something we need to choose again and again and again. As Weil says, "Love is a direction ... not a state of soul."[29] It is a journey of faithfulness, not a once-and-for-all choice. Right now I can say my "nuptial yes" to you and to the heart of your family and the human family and the earth and in another twenty seconds I need to do it again. You, too, need to do the same, again and again and again. How shall we support one another in this direction of soul? What are the shared commitments, rituals, and disciplines that can enable us to do this one thing that is necessary, to love?

> To choose love is not something we do once. It is something we need to choose again and again and again.

Simone Weil was diagnosed with tuberculosis in April 1943 and died at a sanatorium in Ashford, Kent, on August 24, 1943. She was only thirty-four. She had no family with her and, although she had been working for the French Resistance, she was pretty much unknown in Britain, simply getting on with living her "nuptial yes" for her people, and enduring all sorts of personal discomfort and poor health. But to hold up Weil as a prophet and hero of love is not to overdramatize her way. It is not to say that this is everyone's way of loving. Some of us may be called to offer acts of endurance that will be celebrated in generations to come. But most of us are simply called to the much more hidden, and at times entirely overlooked, realm of love in family life, workplace, and the so-called common relationships of day-to-day life.

There is no indication that Weil thought her particular sacrifice would be remembered by others in years to come. She was simply following her direction of soul in ways that she knew how to and could do. This is exactly what each one of us is called to. The poet Mary Oliver, in reflecting on the beauty but apparent insignificance of individual flowers, writes of a rose she is admiring. She speaks of the rose unfolding with its "huge willingness to give something, from its small self, to the entirety of the world."[30] It is this huge willingness that we are being asked to give. This is not to inflate our small self. It is just to say that this is what we have to offer, our small self, and we can offer it with huge willingness.

The final stop on our Iona pilgrimage is St. Martin's Cross. When we gather here, we usually stand in a circle around the cross and recommit ourselves to the way of love. St. Martin's Cross on Iona has a unique feature, and, as far as I know, it is a feature that does not occur in any other high-standing cross in the world. At the heart of the cross on one side, within its circle of oneness, is an image of the Mother and Child. She is holding the babe on her knee and suckling him at her breast. An image of love in its ineffability, and an image that points to the mother's capacity and willingness to labor in birth and nurture the newborn with her own body. Perhaps it is the image that belongs at the very heart of this book. For it invites us to be part of sacred birthing in the world and to nurture it with our body, mind, and soul. We have the capacity to do this. We are made as a means to love. It is God-given. The question is whether we will live what we truly are—love.

Epilogue

At the end of our pilgrimage, after we have stood together in a circle around St. Martin's Cross and committed ourselves again to
the way of love, we walk along a small section of what remains of the
ancient Street of the Dead. It is a centuries-old pathway paved with
sea-rounded stones that have been further smoothed by the feet of
countless pilgrims over the ages. At one time it stretched all the way
from the shores of Iona, where the bodies of Scottish royalty were
brought for burial on the sacred island, to the graveyard called the
Reilig Odhráin that surrounds St. Oran's Chapel. All that is left of it
now is a little stretch of pathway that connects St. Martin's Cross to the
ancient burial ground of St. Oran's.

Walking the Street of the Dead helps us make the connection
between the birthings that we are longing for and the way of dying
or letting go that is implicit in every journey of new beginnings. The
universe continues to unfold because its old formations die to make
way for the ever-new. This is the history of every galaxy, as it is of the
earth and every species, of our nations and families, and the individual
journeys of our lives. The old dissolves to make way for what has never
been before. Or, as we have already heard Jesus saying, "Unless a grain
of wheat falls into the earth and dies, it remains just a single grain; but
if it dies, it bears much fruit" (John 12:24).

What is the dying we are called to be part of if there is to be deep
rebirthing in our lives and our world? What is it we need to let go of
to make room for the new? Specifically, in our Christian household,
how is God to be reborn among us in the many reconnections we have
been considering—with the earth, the way of compassion, seeing the

Light in all things, the journey with other faiths, spiritual practice, nonviolence, accessing the unconscious, and recommitting ourselves to love?

Thomas Berry says, in relation to reconnecting with the earth, that our challenge is "to convert religion to the world rather than to convert the world to religion."[1] What is needed is a conversion to the sacredness of matter and a spiritual communion with the earth. For this to happen, we need to die to the ways in which we have divorced spirit from matter, heaven from earth, eternity from the universe. Jesus says, "You must be born anew" (John 3:7). Rebirth will happen when we fall in love again with the earth.

Aung San Suu Kyi says of the way of compassion that what we need is a "revolution of the spirit."[2] For that revolution to happen in our lives, whether as individuals, nations, or religious traditions, we need to return to the true heart of compassion. In particular, we need to reclaim the courage to compassionately bear responsibility for the needs of others. This means we need to die to the ways we have limited compassion within the narrow confines of our own families, nations, and species. Jesus says, "You must be born anew." Rebirth will mean the waters of compassion breaking open within us again.

Mary Oliver says of the way of awareness that we need to learn "to be astonished."[3] We need to see the Light that is within all life the way a child views the brightness of a new day with open-eyed wonder. We need to see with radical amazement the almost unbelievable gift of every moment. For this to happen we need to die to the calloused ways in which we handle the so-called ordinary encounters of everyday life. Jesus says, "You must be born anew." Rebirth will happen when we see again the glowing luminosity of the numinous in each created thing.

Bede Griffiths says of the way of relationship with other faiths that we need to stop living from only "one half of our soul."[4] We need to open to the treasure of wisdom in traditions other than our own. Not only have they much to teach us, but they also hold the key to unlocking depths within our own religious inheritance that we know nothing of as yet.[5] Jesus says, "You must be born anew." Rebirth means letting go of the cords of confinement so that newborn vision may emerge.

Thomas Merton says of the way of spiritual practice that we need to be turned completely inside out.[6] We need to discover our true meaning not from the outside but from within, so that we can be freed from the false definitions of self that are imposed upon us by cultural norms and expectations. We need to experience our diamond essence again and again if we are to be strong for the holy work of healing the world. But for this to happen we need to die to the many ways in which our ego claims to be the true center of our being. Jesus says, "You must be born anew." Rebirth means engaging in a depth of spiritual practice that will keep liberating our true nature and the deep passions for transformation that lie within us.

Mahatma Gandhi says of the way of nonviolence that we need to reconnect with soul-force rather than brute-force if the relationships of our lives and our world are to be transformed. The work of nonviolence, he said, is like the travail of a new birth.[7] But it will happen only when we die to our excessive reliance on military force and physical might over one another as individuals and nations. Jesus says, "You must be born anew." Rebirth means digging deep into the powerhouse of the soul to effect real change in the world.

Carl Jung says of reconnecting to the unconscious that the universe within is equivalent to the universe without. It is infinite, and there are hidden depths in the inner realm of the soul that we know nothing of yet. These depths are waiting to come forth further and further into the light of our consciousness. Christianity, he says, has led us into the territory of the soul, but "it has not penetrated deeply enough below the surface."[8] We need to die to the ways in which we have been content to stop short at the myths and religious formulations of the past. Jesus says, "You must be born anew." Rebirth will mean a faithful letting go to the imaginal realms of the unconscious so that we can help dream the way forward for the earth.

And Simone Weil says of the way of love that this, above all else, is what we need to reconnect to. For love is the true sacrament of well-being. As lovers "love each other so much that they enter into each other and only make one being," she says, so we are to love the universe, so we are to express our oneness with passion.[9] But for this to happen we need to die to the narrowness of our self-loves, whether as individuals, as nations, or as a species. We need to abandon the blinding illusions of separateness. Jesus says, "You must be born anew." Rebirth will mean a resurrection of love.

Our Christianity "slumbers," says Jung.[10] It is like a great giant who has fallen into the stupor of deep sleep. Its mighty energies for good often lie dormant. When it does stir, as if half remembering the enormity of its strengths, it too often stumbles into irrelevancies and half-truths that are more like a nightmare than a real awakening. Perhaps it is truer to say that Christianity as we have known it is not simply slumbering, it is dying and will be no more. But whether it is a deep slumber, from which we need to awaken, or a death, from which we need the radicalness of resurrection, there is a desperate yearning among us for new beginnings.

In this uncertain time, there are signs of what a reawakened Christianity might look like. Whether they come as if from a dream within our household's slumber or from an even deeper place, from the realm of death where the only thing to do is let go to the Mystery from whom we have come, there is a new vision emerging. And in it we can trace the features of a reborn Christianity. We can see that there will be a reconnecting to the earth, a reclaiming of compassion, a revisioning of Light, a recommitment to the shared journey of faiths, a rediscovery of spiritual practice, a rededication to nonviolence, a reentering of the unconscious, and a reuniting with love. "You must be born anew," says Jesus. It is the coming forth again of what is deepest in us. It is the rebirthing of God.

Notes

Introduction

1. Julian of Norwich, *Revelations of Divine Love*, translated by E. Spearing (London: Penguin, 1998), 129.

2. Ibid., 83.

3. C. G. Jung, *Memories, Dreams, Reflections* (New York: Vintage, 1989), 39.

4. Thomas Berry, *The Sacred Universe: Earth, Spirituality and Religion in the Twenty-First Century* (New York: Columbia University Press, 2009), 133.

5. Aung San Suu Kyi, *Freedom from Fear and Other Writings* (London: Penguin, 1995), 222.

6. Mary Oliver, "When I Am among the Trees," *Thirst* (Boston: Beacon Press, 2006), 4.

7. Bede Griffiths, *The Marriage of East and West* (London: Fount, 1983), 8.

8. Ibid.

9. Thomas Merton, *Contemplative Prayer* (London: Darton, Longman and Todd, 1973), 84.

10. M. K. Gandhi, *An Autobiography: The Story of My Experiments with Truth* (London: Penguin, 1982), 404.

11. C. G. Jung, *The Archetypes and the Collective Unconscious* (London: Routledge, 1990), 40.

12. Simone Weil, *Waiting on God*, translated by E. Craufurd (London: Fontana, 1959), 91.

13. J. P. Newell, *Listening for the Heartbeat of God: A Celtic Spirituality* (London: SPCK, 1997).

Chapter 1: Reconnecting with the Earth

1. Julian of Norwich, *Revelations of Divine Love*, translated by E. Spearing (London: Penguin, 1998), 129.

2. Many of the themes and images developed in this chapter are explored at greater length in previous books by the author. See J. P. Newell's *Book of Creation* (New York: Paulist Press, 1999), *Christ of the Celts: The Healing of Creation* (San Francisco: Jossey-Bass, 2008), and *A New Harmony: The Spirit, The Earth, and the Human Soul* (San Francisco: Jossey-Bass, 2011).

3. David Bohm, *Wholeness and the Implicate Order* (London: Routledge, 1980), xv.

4. John Scotus Eriugena, *Periphyseon*, translated by J. O'Meara (Montreal: Bellarmin, 1987), 293.

5. Ibid., 29.

6. Bohm, *Wholeness*, 11.

7. Brian Swimme and Mary Evelyn Tucker, *Journey of the Universe* (London: Yale University Press, 2011), 71.

8. J. K. Elliot, ed., *The Apocryphal New Testament* (Oxford, UK: Oxford University Press, 1999), 319.

9. Pierre Teilhard de Chardin, *The Heart of Matter*, translated by R. Hague (London: Collins, 1978), 15.

10. Pierre Teilhard de Chardin, *Christianity and Evolution*, translated by R. Hague (London: Collins, 1971), 128.

11. Pierre Teilhard de Chardin, *The Prayer of the Universe*, translated by R. Hague (London: Collins, 1977), 143.

12. Ibid., 89.

13. Teilhard de Chardin, *Christianity and Evolution*, 94.

14. Ibid., 95.

15. Teilhard de Chardin, *Prayer of the Universe*, 88.

16. Ibid., 86.

17. Ibid., 41.

18. Pierre Teilhard de Chardin, *Le Milieu Divin*, translated by R. Hague (London: Collins, 1967), 154.

19. Walter Schwartz, "Thomas Berry Obituary," September 27, 2009; www.guardian.co.uk/world/2009/sep/27/thomas-berry-obituary (accessed April 6, 2012).

20. Thomas Berry, *The Great Work* (New York: Bell Tower, 1999), ix.

21. Ibid., 164.

22. Thomas Berry, *The Sacred Universe* (New York: Columbia University Press, 2009), 133.

23. Ibid., 69.

24. Berry, *Great Work*, 201.

25. Ibid.

Chapter 2: Reconnecting with Compassion

1. Aung San Suu Kyi, *The Voice of Hope*, edited by A. Clements (London: Rider, 2008), 10.
2. Ibid., 161.
3. Ibid., 41.
4. Ibid., pp. 11–12.
5. Aung San Suu Kyi, *Freedom from Fear* (London: Penguin, 1995), 174.
6. Aung San Suu Kyi, *Letters from Burma* (London: Penguin, 2010), 56.
7. Suu Kyi, *Voice of Hope*, 94.
8. Ibid., 98.
9. Suu Kyi, *Freedom from Fear*, 243.
10. Ibid., 222.
11. Ibid.
12. Ibid., 247.
13. Suu Kyi, *Voice of Hope*, 165, 181.
14. Suu Kyi, *Freedom from Fear*, 243.
15. Suu Kyi, *Voice of Hope*, 44.
16. Ibid., 12.
17. Ibid., 43.
18. Suu Kyi, *Freedom from Fear*, 229.
19. Suu Kyi, *Voice of Hope*, 124.
20. Suu Kyi, *Freedom from Fear*, 212.
21. Suu Kyi, *Voice of Hope*, 221.
22. Ibid., 7.
23. Ibid., 127.
24. Ibid., 90.

Chapter 3: Reconnecting with the Light

1. George F. MacLeod, *The Whole Earth Shall Cry Glory*, edited by R. Ferguson (Glasgow: Wild Goose Publications, 1985), 16.
2. Mary Oliver, "The Sun," in *New and Selected Poems*, vol. 1 (Boston: Beacon Press, 1992), 50–51.
3. Mary Oliver, "Six Recognitions of the Lord," in *Thirst* (Boston: Beacon Press, 2006), 26–27.
4. MacLeod, *Whole Earth Shall Cry Glory*, 60.

5. Mary Oliver, "The Black Snake," in *New and Selected Poems*, vol. 1, 184.

6. Mary Oliver, "The Ponds," in *New and Selected Poems*, vol. 1, 93.

7. John Scotus Eriugena, *Periphyseon*, translated by J. O'Meara (Montreal: Bellarmin, 1987), 116.

8. Ibid., 38.

9. Kenneth White, "The House of Insight," in *The Bird Path: Collected Longer Poems* (Edinburgh: Mainstream Publishing, 1989), 145.

10. Mary Oliver, "Messenger," in *Thirst*, 1.

11. Mary Oliver, "Praying," in *Thirst*, 37.

12. Eriugena, *Periphyseon*, 308.

13. Mary Oliver, "On Thy Wondrous Works I Will Meditate," in *Thirst*, 57.

14. Mary Oliver, "When I Am Among the Trees," in *Thirst*, 4.

15. John Muir, "My First Summer in the Sierra," in *Nature Writings* (New York: Library of America, 1997), 237.

16. Mary Oliver, "When Death Comes," in *New and Selected Poems*, vol. 1, 10.

17. Mary Oliver, "Wild Geese," in *New and Selected Poems*, vol. 1, 110.

18. Mary Oliver, "The Family," in *New and Selected Poems*, vol. 1, 215.

19. P. Ackroyd, *Blake* (New York: Ballantine Books, 1995), 34.

20. Mary Oliver, "In Blackwater Woods," in *American Primitive* (Boston: Back Bay Books, 1983), 83.

21. Mary Oliver, "October," in *New and Selected Poems*, vol. 1, 60.

22. Mary Oliver, "When Death Comes," in *New and Selected Poems*, vol. 1, 10–11.

Chapter 4: Reconnecting with the Journey

1. Julian of Norwich, *Revelations of Divine Love*, translated by E. Spearing (London: Penguin, 1998), 129.

2. Peter Berresford Ellis, *A Brief History of the Druids* (Philadelphia: Running Press, 2002), 79.

3. Nora Chadwick, *The Celts* (London: Penguin Books, 1971), 206.

4. Thomas Berry, *The Christian Future and the Fate of the Earth* (New York: Orbis Books, 2009), 21.

5. Bede Griffiths, *The Marriage of East and West* (London: Fount, 1983), 8.

6. Shirley Du Boulay, *Beyond the Darkness: A Biography of Bede Griffiths* (London: Rider, 1998), 206.

7. Ibid., 139.

8. Ibid., 88.

9. Griffiths, *Marriage of East and West*, 8.

10. Meister Eckhart, *Teacher and Preacher*, translated by B. McGinn (Mahwah, NJ: Paulist Press, 1986), 54.

11. John Philip Newell, *A New Harmony: The Spirit, the Earth, and the Human Soul* (San Francisco: Jossey-Bass, 2011), 25–28, 42–45.

12. Du Boulay, *Beyond the Darkness*, 228.

Chapter 5: Reconnecting with Spiritual Practice

1. Thomas Merton, *Contemplative Prayer* (London: Darton, Longman, and Todd, 1973), 142.

2. Jim Forest, *Living with Wisdom: A Life of Thomas Merton* (Maryknoll, NY: Orbis Books, 2008), 184.

3. Merton, *Contemplative Prayer*, 98.

4. Ibid., 82.

5. Thomas Merton, *The Asian Journal of Thomas Merton* (New York: New Directions Books, 1975), 349.

6. From Carl Jung's interview with John Freeman in the BBC's *Face to Face* series, 1959.

7. Ibid.

8. Forest, *Living with Wisdom*, 134.

9. Ibid., 134.

10. Merton, *Contemplative Prayer*, 34.

11. Ibid., 84.

12. Ibid.

13. Ibid., 43.

14. Ibid., 112.

15. Ibid., 50.

16. Edwin Muir, *Collected Poems* (London: Faber and Faber, 1984), 240.

17. Merton, *Contemplative Prayer*, 111.

18. Ibid., 83.

19. Forest, *Living with Wisdom*, 134.

20. Ibid., 147.

21. Merton, *Contemplative Prayer*, 25.

22. Forest, *Living with Wisdom*, 116.

23. Ibid.

24. Ibid., 133.

25. Ibid., 134.

26. Ibid., 203.

27. Merton, *Asian Journal*, 316.

28. Ibid., 308.

29. Merton, *Contemplative Prayer*, 85.

30. Ibid., 28.

31. Ibid., 89.

32. Forest, *Living with Wisdom*, 173.

33. Ibid., 178.

34. Merton, *Contemplative Prayer*, 137.

35. Ibid., 86.

36. Merton, *Asian Journal*, 350.

37. Ibid.

38. Merton, *Contemplative Prayer*, 126.

Chapter 6: Reconnecting with Nonviolence

1. George F. MacLeod, *The Whole Earth Shall Cry Glory*, edited by R. Ferguson (Glasgow: Wild Goose Publications, 1985), 45.

2. Louis Fischer, *The Life of Mahatma Gandhi* (London: Harper Collins, 1997), 416.

3. Louis Fischer, ed., *The Essential Gandhi* (New York: Vintage Spiritual Classics, 2002), 80.

4. Fischer, *Life of Mahatma Gandhi*, 526.

5. Fischer, *Essential Gandhi*, 290.

6. M. K. Gandhi, *An Autobiography: The Story of My Experiments with Truth* (London: Penguin, 1982), 404.

7. Fischer, *Essential Gandhi*, 190.

8. Gandhi, *Autobiography*, 404.

9. Fischer, *Essential Gandhi*, 294.

10. Ibid., 190.

11. Gandhi, *Autobiography*, 254.

12. Fischer, *Essential Gandhi*, 145.

13. Ibid., 248.

14. Ibid., 161.

15. Fischer, *Life of Mahatma Gandhi*, 416.

16. Fischer, *The Essential Gandhi*, 184.

17. Ibid.

18. Ibid., 198.

19. Ibid., 269.

20. Fischer, *Life of Mahatma Gandhi*, 380.

21. Fischer, *Essential Gandhi*, 225.

22. Gandhi, *Autobiography*, 81.

23. Fischer, *Essential Gandhi*, 179.

24. Gandhi, *Autobiography*, 454.

25. MacLeod, *The Whole Earth Shall Cry Glory*, 13–14.

26. Ibid., 60 (slightly adapted by the author).

Chapter 7: Reconnecting with the Unconscious

1. C. G. Jung, *The Archetypes and the Collective Unconscious* (London: Routledge, 1990), 24.

2. C. G. Jung, *Memories, Dreams, Reflections* (New York: Vintage, 1989), 138.

3. Ibid., 193.

4. C. G. Jung, *Aion* (Princeton, NJ: Princeton University Press, 1979), 254.

5. C. G. Jung, *Mysterium Coniunctionis* (Princeton, NJ: Princeton University Press, 1989), 148, 180.

6. C. G. Jung, *Psychology and Religion* (Princeton, NJ: Princeton University Press, 1975), 186.

7. Jung, *Mysterium Coniunctionis*, 156.

8. Jung, *Aion*, 268.

9. Ibid.

10. Jung, *Memories, Dreams, Reflections*, 337.

11. See Ken Wilber, *No Boundary* (Boston: Shambhala, 1985).

12. Jung, *Mysterium Coniunctionis*, 364.

13. Jung, *Memories, Dreams, Reflections*, 40.

14. Jung, *The Archetypes and the Collective Unconscious*, 164.

15. Anthony de Mello, *Wellsprings* (New York: Doubleday, 1986), 219.

16. From a telephone interview with Oscar Romero by Mexican journalist, José Calderon Salazar, correspondent of *Excelsior* newspaper, two weeks before Romero's assassination on March 24, 1980, www.romerotrust.org.uk (accessed December 12, 2013).

17. Jung, *Mysterium Coniunctionis*, 375.

Chapter 8: Reconnecting with Love

1. C. G. Jung, *Memories, Dreams, Reflections* (New York: Vintage, 1989), 353.

2. Ibid., 354.

3. Ibid.

4. C. G. Jung, *Mysterium Coniunctionis* (Princeton, NJ: Princeton University Press, 1989), 101.

5. B. Gillman, "Bind Us Together" (London: Kingsway Communications, 1974), www.worshiptogether.com.

6. John Hellman, *Simone Weil: An Introduction to Her Thought* (Waterloo, ON: Wilfrid Laurier University Press, 1983), 1.

7. Simone Weil, *Waiting on God*, translated by E. Craufurd (London: Fontana, 1959), 83.

8. Ibid., 82.

9. Ibid., 91.

10. Ibid., 92.

11. Ibid., 62.

12. Ibid., 60.

13. Ibid., 132.

14. Ibid.

15. Simone Weil, *An Anthology*, edited by S. Miles (London: Penguin, 2005), 292.

16. Ibid., 34.

17. Ibid., 232.

18. Ibid., 233.

19. Weil, *Waiting on God*, 41.

20. Ibid., 130.

21. Ibid., 115.

22. Ibid.

23. Ibid., 168.

24. Ibid., 150.

25. Ibid., 97.

26. Weil, *Anthology*, 212.

27. Weil, *Waiting on God*, 100, 115.

28. Martin Buber, *The Letters of Martin Buber: A Life of Dialogue*, edited by N. Glatzer (Syracuse, NY: Syracuse University Press, 1996), 499.

29. Weil, *Waiting on God*, 93.

30. Mary Oliver, "The Poet Visits the Museum of Fine Arts," in *Thirst* (Boston: Beacon Press, 2006), 5.

Epilogue

1. Thomas Berry, *The Sacred Universe* (New York: Columbia University Press, 2009), 12.

2. Alan Clements, ed., *The Voice of Hope: Aung San Suu Kyi* (London: Rider, 2008), 10.

3. Mary Oliver, "Messenger," in *Thirst* (Boston: Beacon Press, 2006), 1.

4. Bede Griffiths, *The Marriage of East and West* (London: Fount, 1983), 8.

5. Shirley du Boulay, *Beyond the Darkness: A Biography of Bede Griffiths* (London: Rider, 1998), 181.

6. Thomas Merton, *Contemplative Prayer* (London: Darton, Longman and Todd, 1973), 137.

7. Louis Fischer, ed., *The Essential Gandhi* (New York: Vintage Spiritual Classics, 2002), 177.

8. C. G. Jung, *The Archetypes and the Collective Unconscious* (London: Routledge, 1990), 254.

9. Simone Weil, *Waiting on God*, translated by E. Craufurd (London: Fontana, 1959), 85.

10. C. G. Jung, *Memories, Dreams, Reflections* (New York: Vintage, 1989), 331.

Suggestions for Further Reading

Aung San Suu Kyi. *The Voice of Hope*. Edited by Alan Clements. London: Rider Books, 2008.

Berry, Thomas. *The Great Work: Our Way Into the Future*. New York: Broadway, 2000.

Ferguson, Ron. *George MacLeod: Founder of the Iona Community*. Glasgow: Wild Goose Publications, 2004.

Gandhi, M. K. *An Autobiography: The Story of My Experiments with Truth*. Boston: Beacon Press, 1993.

Griffiths, Bede. *The Marriage of East and West*. Springfield, IL: Templegate Publishers, 1982.

Jung, C. G. *Memories, Dreams, Reflections*. New York: Vintage, 1989.

MacArthur, Mairi. *Columba's Island: Iona from Past to Present*. Edinburgh: Edinburgh University Press, 2007.

Merton, Thomas. *Contemplative Prayer*. London: Darton, Longman, and Todd, 1973.

Newell, John Philip. *Christ of the Celts: The Healing of Creation*. San Francisco: Jossey-Bass, 2008.

———. *Listening for the Heartbeat of God: A Celtic Spirituality*. New York: Paulist Press, 1997.

———. *A New Harmony: The Spirit, the Earth, and the Human Soul*. San Francisco: Jossey-Bass, 2011.

Oliver, Mary. *New and Selected Poems* (Volume 1). Boston: Beacon Press, 1992.

Teilhard de Chardin, Pierre. *The Divine Milieu*. New York: Harper Perennial, 2001.

Weil, Simone. *Waiting for God*. New York: Harper Perennial, 2009.

About the Author

The Reverend Dr. John Philip Newell is a poet, peacemaker, and scholar. In 2011 he received the first-ever Contemplative Voices Award from the Shalem Institute in Washington, D.C. He divides his time between Edinburgh in Scotland with his family, where he does most of his writing, and the United States, where he teaches and preaches across the nation. Formerly warden of Iona Abbey in the Western Isles of Scotland, he is now companion theologian for the American Spirituality Center of Casa del Sol at Ghost Ranch in the high desert of New Mexico, where he and his wife spend their summers. Newell, the cofounder of Heartbeat: A Journey Towards Earth's Wellbeing, is an ordained Church of Scotland minister with a passion for peace among the great wisdom traditions of humanity. His doctorate is from the University of Edinburgh and he is internationally recognized for his work in the field of Celtic spirituality, having authored over fifteen books, including *Listening for the Heartbeat of God*, *Praying with the Earth*, and his highly acclaimed visionary work *A New Harmony: The Spirit, the Earth & the Human Soul*. For more information about the author, visit his website at www.heartbeatjourney.org.

Inspiration

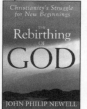

The Rebirthing of God
Christianity's Struggle for New Beginnings
By John Philip Newell
Drawing on modern prophets from East and West, and using the holy island of Iona as an icon of new beginnings, Celtic poet, peacemaker and scholar John Philip Newell dares us to imagine a new birth from deep within Christianity, a fresh stirring of the Spirit.
6 x 9, 160 pp, HC, 978-1-59473-542-4 **$19.99**

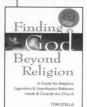

Finding God Beyond Religion: A Guide for Skeptics, Agnostics & Unorthodox Believers Inside & Outside the Church
By Tom Stella; Foreword by The Rev. Canon Marianne Wells Borg
Reinterprets traditional religious teachings central to the Christian faith for people who have outgrown the beliefs and devotional practices that once made sense to them.
6 x 9, 160 pp, Quality PB, 978-1-59473-485-4 **$16.99**

Fully Awake and Truly Alive: Spiritual Practices to Nurture Your Soul
By Rev. Jane E. Vennard; Foreword by Rami Shapiro
Illustrates the joys and frustrations of spiritual practice, offers insights from various religious traditions and provides exercises and meditations to help us become more fully alive.
6 x 9, 208 pp, Quality PB, 978-1-59473-473-1 **$16.99**

Journeys of Simplicity: Traveling Light with Thomas Merton, Bashō, Edward Abbey, Annie Dillard & Others   *By Philip Harnden*
Invites you to consider a more graceful way of traveling through life. PB includes journal pages to help you get started on your own spiritual journey.
5½ x 7¼, 144 pp, Quality PB, 978-1-59473-181-5 **$12.99**
5½ x 7¼, 128 pp, HC, 978-1-893361-76-8 **$16.95**

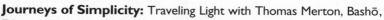

Perennial Wisdom for the Spiritually Independent
Sacred Teachings—Annotated & Explained
Annotation by Rami Shapiro; Foreword by Richard Rohr
Weaves sacred texts and teachings from the world's major religions into a coherent exploration of the five core questions at the heart of every religion's search.
5½ x 8½, 336 pp, Quality PB Original, 978-1-59473-515-8 **$16.99**

Saving Civility: 52 Ways to Tame Rude, Crude & Attitude for a Polite Planet
By Sara Hacala
Provides fifty-two practical ways you can reverse the course of incivility and make the world a more enriching, pleasant place to live.
6 x 9, 240 pp, Quality PB, 978-1-59473-314-7 **$16.99**

Spiritually Healthy Divorce: Navigating Disruption with Insight & Hope
By Carolyne Call
A spiritual map to help you move through the twists and turns of divorce.
6 x 9, 224 pp, Quality PB, 978-1-59473-288-1 **$16.99**

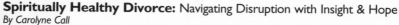

Or phone, fax, mail or email to: SKYLIGHT PATHS Publishing
Sunset Farm Offices, Route 4 • P.O. Box 237 • Woodstock, Vermont 05091
Tel: (802) 457-4000 • Fax: (802) 457-4004 • www.skylightpaths.com
Credit card orders: (800) 962-4544 (8:30AM–5:30PM EST Monday–Friday)
Generous discounts on quantity orders. SATISFACTION GUARANTEED. Prices subject to change.

Sacred Texts—SkyLight Illuminations Series

Offers today's spiritual seeker an enjoyable entry into the great classic texts of the world's spiritual traditions. Each classic is presented in an accessible translation, with facing pages of guided commentary from experts, giving you the keys you need to understand the history, context and meaning of the text.

CHRISTIANITY

The Book of Common Prayer: A Spiritual Treasure Chest—Selections Annotated & Explained

Annotation by The Rev. Canon C. K. Robertson, PhD; Foreword by The Most Rev. Katharine Jefferts Schori; Preface by Archbishop Desmond Tutu

Makes available the riches of this spiritual treasure chest for all who are interested in deepening their life of prayer, building stronger relationships and making a difference in their world. 5½ x 8½. 208 pp, Quality PB Original, 978-1-59473-524-0 **$16.99**

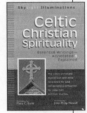

Celtic Christian Spirituality: Essential Writings—Annotated & Explained

Annotation by Mary C. Earle; Foreword by John Philip Newell

Explores how the writings of this lively tradition embody the gospel.
5½ x 8½, 176 pp, Quality PB, 978-1-59473-302-4 **$16.99**

Desert Fathers and Mothers: Early Christian Wisdom Sayings—Annotated & Explained *Annotation by Christine Valters Paintner, PhD*

Opens up wisdom of the desert fathers and mothers for readers with no previous knowledge of Western monasticism and early Christianity.
5½ x 8½, 192 pp, Quality PB, 978-1-59473-373-4 **$16.99**

The End of Days: Essential Selections from Apocalyptic Texts—Annotated & Explained *Annotation by Robert G. Clouse, PhD*

Helps you understand the complex Christian visions of the end of the world.
5½ x 8½, 224 pp, Quality PB, 978-1-59473-170-9 **$16.99**

The Hidden Gospel of Matthew: Annotated & Explained

Translation & Annotation by Ron Miller

Discover the words and events that have the strongest connection to the historical Jesus.
5½ x 8½, 272 pp, Quality PB, 978-1-59473-038-2 **$16.99**

The Imitation of Christ: Selections Annotated & Explained

Annotation by Paul Wesley Chilcote, PhD; By Thomas à Kempis; Adapted from John Wesley's The Christian's Pattern

Let Jesus's example of holiness, humility and purity of heart be a companion on your own spiritual journey.
5½ x 8½, 224 pp, Quality PB, 978-1-59473-434-2 **$16.99**

The Infancy Gospels of Jesus: Apocryphal Tales from the Childhoods of Mary and Jesus—Annotated & Explained

Translation & Annotation by Stevan Davies; Foreword by A. Edward Siecienski, PhD

A startling presentation of the early lives of Mary, Jesus and other biblical figures that will amuse and surprise you. 5½ x 8½, 176 pp, Quality PB, 978-1-59473-258-4 **$16.99**

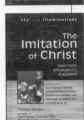

John & Charles Wesley: Selections from Their Writings and Hymns—Annotated & Explained *Annotation by Paul W. Chilcote, PhD*

A unique presentation of the writings of these two inspiring brothers brings together some of the most essential material from their large corpus of work.
5½ x 8½, 288 pp, Quality PB, 978-1-59473-309-3 **$16.99**

Julian of Norwich: Selections from *Revelations of Divine Love*—Annotated & Explained *Annotation by Mary C. Earle*

Addresses topics including the infinite nature of God, the life of prayer, God's suffering with us, the eternal and undying life of the soul, the motherhood of Jesus and the motherhood of God and more.
5½ x 8½, 224 pp, Quality PB Original, 978-1-59473-513-4 **$16.99**

Sacred Texts—continued

CHRISTIANITY—continued

The Lost Sayings of Jesus: Teachings from Ancient Christian, Jewish, Gnostic and Islamic Sources—Annotated & Explained
Translation & Annotation by Andrew Phillip Smith; Foreword by Stephan A. Hoeller
Depicts Jesus as a Wisdom teacher who speaks to people of all faiths as a mystic and spiritual master. 5½ x 8½, 240 pp, Quality PB, 978-1-59473-172-3 **$16.99**

Philokalia: The Eastern Christian Spiritual Texts—Selections Annotated & Explained *Annotation by Allyne Smith; Translation by G. E. H. Palmer, Phillip Sherrard and Bishop Kallistos Ware* The first approachable introduction to the wisdom of the Philokalia. 5½ x 8½, 240 pp, Quality PB, 978-1-59473-103-7 **$18.99**

The Sacred Writings of Paul: Selections Annotated & Explained
Translation & Annotation by Ron Miller Leads you into the exciting immediacy of Paul's teachings. 5½ x 8½, 224 pp, Quality PB, 978-1-59473-213-3 **$16.99**

Saint Augustine of Hippo: Selections from *Confessions* and Other Essential Writings—Annotated & Explained
Annotation by Joseph T. Kelley, PhD; Translation by the Augustinian Heritage Institute
Provides insight into the mind and heart of this foundational Christian figure.
5½ x 8½, 272 pp, Quality PB, 978-1-59473-282-9 **$16.99**

Saint Ignatius Loyola—The Spiritual Writings: Selections Annotated & Explained *Annotation by Mark Mossa, SJ* Focuses on the practical mysticism of Ignatius of Loyola. 5½ x 8½, 288 pp, Quality PB, 978-1-59473-301-7 **$18.99**

Sex Texts from the Bible: Selections Annotated & Explained
Translation & Annotation by Teresa J. Hornsby; Foreword by Amy-Jill Levine
Demystifies the Bible's ideas on gender roles, marriage, sexual orientation, virginity, lust and sexual pleasure. 5½ x 8½, 208 pp, Quality PB, 978-1-59473-217-1 **$16.99**

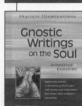

Spiritual Writings on Mary: Annotated & Explained
Annotation by Mary Ford-Grabowsky; Foreword by Andrew Harvey
Examines the role of Mary, the mother of Jesus, as a source of inspiration in history and in life today. 5½ x 8½, 272 pp, Quality PB, 978-1-59473-001-6 **$16.99**

The Way of a Pilgrim: The Jesus Prayer Journey—Annotated & Explained
Translation & Annotation by Gleb Pokrovsky; Foreword by Andrew Harvey A classic of Russian Orthodox spirituality. 5½ x 8½, 160 pp, Illus., Quality PB, 978-1-893361-31-7 **$15.99**

GNOSTICISM

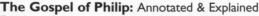

Gnostic Writings on the Soul: Annotated & Explained
Translation & Annotation by Andrew Phillip Smith; Foreword by Stephan A. Hoeller
Reveals the inspiring ways your soul can remember and return to its unique, divine purpose. 5½ x 8½, 144 pp, Quality PB, 978-1-59473-220-1 **$16.99**

The Gospel of Philip: Annotated & Explained
Translation & Annotation by Andrew Phillip Smith; Foreword by Stevan Davies
Reveals otherwise unrecorded sayings of Jesus and fragments of Gnostic mythology.
5½ x 8½, 160 pp, Quality PB, 978-1-59473-111-2 **$16.99**

The Gospel of Thomas: Annotated & Explained
Translation & Annotation by Stevan Davies; Foreword by Andrew Harvey
Sheds new light on the origins of Christianity and portrays Jesus as a wisdom-loving sage.
5½ x 8½, 192 pp, Quality PB, 978-1-893361-45-4 **$16.99**

The Secret Book of John: The Gnostic Gospel—Annotated & Explained
Translation & Annotation by Stevan Davies The most significant and influential text of the ancient Gnostic religion. 5½ x 8½, 208 pp, Quality PB, 978-1-59473-082-5 **$18.99**

See Inspiration for *Perennial Wisdom for the Spiritually Independent: Sacred Teachings—Annotated & Explained*

Spirituality

The Forgiveness Handbook
Spiritual Wisdom and Practice for the Journey to Freedom, Healing and Peace
Created by the Editors at SkyLight Paths; Introduction by The Rev. Canon Marianne Wells Borg
Offers inspiration, encouragement and spiritual practice from across faith traditions for all who seek hope, wholeness and the freedom that comes from true forgiveness.
6 x 9, 256 pp, Quality PB, 978-1-59473-577-6 **$18.99**

Like a Child
Restoring the Awe, Wonder, Joy and Resiliency of the Human Spirit
By Rev. Timothy J. Mooney
By breaking free from our misperceptions about what it means to be an adult, we can reshape our world and become harbingers of grace. This unique spiritual resource explores Jesus's counsel to become like children in order to enter the kingdom of God. 6 x 9, 160 pp, Quality PB, 978-1-59473-543-1 **$16.99**

The Passionate Jesus: What We Can Learn from Jesus about Love, Fear, Grief, Joy and Living Authentically
By The Rev. Peter Wallace
Reveals Jesus as a passionate figure who was involved, present, connected, honest and direct with others and encourages you to build personal authenticity in every area of your own life. 6 x 9, 208 pp, Quality PB, 978-1-59473-393-2 **$18.99**

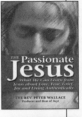

Gathering at God's Table: The Meaning of Mission in the Feast of Faith
By Katharine Jefferts Schori
A profound reminder of our role in the larger frame of God's dream for a restored and reconciled world. 6 x 9, 256 pp, HC, 978-1-59473-316-1 **$21.99**

The Heartbeat of God: Finding the Sacred in the Middle of Everything
By Katharine Jefferts Schori; Foreword by Joan Chittister, OSB
Explores our connections to other people, to other nations and with the environment through the lens of faith.
6 x 9, 240 pp, HC, 978-1-59473-292-8 **$21.99**

A Dangerous Dozen: Twelve Christians Who Threatened the Status Quo but Taught Us to Live Like Jesus
By The Rev. Canon C. K. Robertson, PhD; Foreword by Archbishop Desmond Tutu
Profiles twelve visionary men and women who challenged society and showed the world a different way of living.
6 x 9, 208 pp, Quality PB, 978-1-59473-298-0 **$16.99**

Laugh Your Way to Grace: Reclaiming the Spiritual Power of Humor
By Rev. Susan Sparks
A powerful, humorous case for laughter as a spiritual, healing path.
6 x 9, 176 pp, Quality PB, 978-1-59473-280-5 **$16.99**

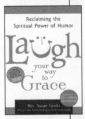

Claiming Earth as Common Ground: The Ecological Crisis through the Lens of Faith
By Andrea Cohen-Kiener; Foreword by Rev. Sally Bingham
6 x 9, 192 pp, Quality PB, 978-1-59473-261-4 **$16.99**

Living into Hope: A Call to Spiritual Action for Such a Time as This
By Rev. Dr. Joan Brown Campbell; Foreword by Karen Armstrong
6 x 9, 208 pp, Quality PB, 978-1-59473-436-6 **$18.99**; HC, 978-1-59473-283-6 **$21.99**

Renewal in the Wilderness
A Spiritual Guide to Connecting with God in the Natural World
By John Lionberger 6 x 9, 176 pp, b/w photos, Quality PB, 978-1-59473-219-5 **$16.99**

Spiritual Adventures in the Snow
Skiing & Snowboarding as Renewal for Your Soul
By Dr. Marcia McFee and Rev. Karen Foster; Foreword by Paul Arthur
5½ x 8½, 208 pp, Quality PB, 978-1-59473-270-6 **$16.99**

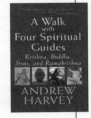

A Walk with Four Spiritual Guides: Krishna, Buddha, Jesus, and Ramakrishna
By Andrew Harvey 5½ x 8½, 192 pp, b/w photos & illus., Quality PB, 978-1-59473-138-9 **$15.99**

Prayer / Meditation

Calling on God
Inclusive Christian Prayers for Three Years of Sundays
By Peter Bankson and Deborah Sokolove
Prayers for today's world, vividly written for Christians who long for a way to talk to and about God that feels fresh yet still connected to tradition.
6 x 9, 400 pp, Quality PB, 978-1-59473-568-4 **$18.99**

Openings, 2nd Edition
A Daybook of Saints, Sages, Psalms and Prayer Practices
By Rev. Larry J. Peacock
For anyone hungry for a richer prayer life, this prayer book offers daily inspiration to help you move closer to God. Draws on a wide variety of resources—lives of saints and sages from every age, psalms, and suggestions for personal reflection and practice. 6 x 9, 448 pp, Quality PB, 978-1-59473-545-5 **$18.99**

Men Pray: Voices of Strength, Faith, Healing, Hope and Courage
Created by the Editors at SkyLight Paths; With Introductions by Brian D. McLaren
Celebrates the rich variety of ways men around the world have called out to the Divine—with words of joy, praise, gratitude, wonder, petition and even anger—from the ancient world up to our own day.
5 x 7¼, 192 pp, HC, 978-1-59473-395-6 **$16.99**

Honest to God Prayer: Spirituality as Awareness, Empowerment,
Relinquishment and Paradox *By Kent Ira Groff*
6 x 9, 192 pp, Quality PB, 978-1-59473-433-5 **$16.99**

Lectio Divina—The Sacred Art
Transforming Words & Images into Heart-Centered Prayer
By Christine Valters Paintner, PhD
5½ x 8½, 240 pp, Quality PB, 978-1-59473-300-0 **$16.99**

Sacred Attention: A Spiritual Practice for Finding God in the Moment
By Margaret D. McGee
6 x 9, 144 pp, Quality PB, 978-1-59473-291-1 **$16.99**

Secrets of Prayer: A Multifaith Guide to Creating Personal Prayer in Your Life
By Nancy Corcoran, CSJ
6 x 9, 160 pp, Quality PB, 978-1-59473-215-7 **$16.99**

Women of Color Pray: Voices of Strength, Faith, Healing, Hope and Courage
Edited and with Introductions by Christal M. Jackson
5 x 7¼, 208 pp, Quality PB, 978-1-59473-077-1 **$15.99**

Prayer / M. Basil Pennington, OCSO

Finding Grace at the Center, 3rd Edition: The Beginning of
Centering Prayer *With Thomas Keating, OCSO, and Thomas E. Clarke, SJ*
Foreword by Rev. Cynthia Bourgeault, PhD A practical guide to a simple and beautiful form of meditative prayer. 5 x 7¼, 128 pp, Quality PB, 978-1-59473-182-2 **$12.99**

The Monks of Mount Athos: A Western Monk's Extraordinary
Spiritual Journey on Eastern Holy Ground *Foreword by Archimandrite Dionysios*
Explores the landscape, monastic communities and food of Athos.
6 x 9, 352 pp, Quality PB, 978-1-893361-78-2 **$18.95**

Psalms: A Spiritual Commentary *Illus. by Phillip Ratner*
Reflections on some of the most beloved passages from the Bible's most widely read book. 6 x 9, 176 pp, 24 full-page b/w illus., Quality PB, 978-1-59473-234-8 **$16.99**

The Song of Songs: A Spiritual Commentary *Illus. by Phillip Ratner*
Explore the Bible's most challenging mystical text.
6 x 9, 160 pp, 14 full-page b/w illus., Quality PB, 978-1-59473-235-5 **$16.99**
HC, 978-1-59473-004-7 **$19.99**

Spiritual Practice—The Sacred Art of Living Series

Dreaming—The Sacred Art: Incubating, Navigating & Interpreting Sacred Dreams for Spiritual & Personal Growth
By Lori Joan Swick
This fascinating introduction to sacred dreams celebrates the dream experience as a way to deepen spiritual awareness and as a source of self-healing. Designed for the novice and the experienced sacred dreamer of all faith traditions, or none.
5½ x 8½, 224 pp, Quality PB, 978-1-59473-544-8 **$16.99**

Conversation—The Sacred Art: Practicing Presence in an Age of Distraction
By Diane M. Millis, PhD; Foreword by Rev. Tilden Edwards, PhD
5½ x 8½, 192 pp, Quality PB, 978-1-59473-474-8 **$16.99**

Dance—The Sacred Art: The Joy of Movement as a Spiritual Practice
By Cynthia Winton-Henry 5½ x 8½, 224 pp, Quality PB, 978-1-59473-268-3 **$16.99**

Fly-Fishing—The Sacred Art: Casting a Fly as a Spiritual Practice
By Rabbi Eric Eisenkramer and Rev. Michael Attas, MD; Foreword by Chris Wood, CEO, Trout Unlimited; Preface by Lori Simon, executive director, Casting for Recovery
5½ x 8½, 160 pp, Quality PB, 978-1-59473-299-7 **$16.99**

Giving—The Sacred Art: Creating a Lifestyle of Generosity
By Lauren Tyler Wright 5½ x 8½, 208 pp, Quality PB, 978-1-59473-224-9 **$16.99**

Haiku—The Sacred Art: A Spiritual Practice in Three Lines
By Margaret D. McGee 5½ x 8½, 192 pp, Quality PB, 978-1-59473-269-0 **$16.99**

Hospitality—The Sacred Art: Discovering the Hidden Spiritual Power of Invitation and Welcome By Rev. Nanette Sawyer; Foreword by Rev. Dirk Ficca
5½ x 8½, 208 pp, Quality PB, 978-1-59473-228-7 **$16.99**

Labyrinths from the Outside In, 2nd Edition: Walking to Spiritual Insight—A Beginner's Guide By Rev. Dr. Donna Schaper and Rev. Dr. Carole Ann Camp
6 x 9, 208 pp, b/w illus. and photos, Quality PB, 978-1-59473-486-1 **$16.99**

Lectio Divina—The Sacred Art
Transforming Words & Images into Heart-Centered Prayer
By Christine Valters Paintner, PhD 5½ x 8½, 240 pp, Quality PB, 978-1-59473-300-0 **$16.99**

Pilgrimage—The Sacred Art: Journey to the Center of the Heart
By Dr. Sheryl A. Kujawa-Holbrook 5½ x 8½, 240 pp, Quality PB, 978-1-59473-472-4 **$16.99**

Practicing the Sacred Art of Listening: A Guide to Enrich Your Relationships and Kindle Your Spiritual Life By Kay Lindahl 8 x 8, 176 pp, Quality PB, 978-1-893361-85-0 **$18.99**

Recovery—The Sacred Art: The Twelve Steps as Spiritual Practice by Rami Shapiro; Foreword by Joan Borysenko, PhD 5½ x 8½, 240 pp, Quality PB, 978-1-59473-259-1 **$16.99**

Running—The Sacred Art: Preparing to Practice By Dr. Warren A. Kay; Foreword by Kristin Armstrong 5½ x 8½, 160 pp, Quality PB, 978-1-59473-227-0 **$16.99**

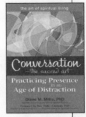

The Sacred Art of Chant: Preparing to Practice
By Ana Hernández 5½ x 8½, 192 pp, Quality PB, 978-1-59473-036-8 **$16.99**

The Sacred Art of Fasting: Preparing to Practice
By Thomas Ryan, CSP 5½ x 8½, 192 pp, Quality PB, 978-1-59473-078-8 **$15.99**

The Sacred Art of Forgiveness: Forgiving Ourselves and Others through God's Grace
By Marcia Ford 8 x 8, 176 pp, Quality PB, 978-1-59473-175-4 **$18.99**

The Sacred Art of Listening: Forty Reflections for Cultivating a Spiritual Practice
By Kay Lindahl; Illus. by Amy Schnapper 8 x 8, 160 pp, b/w illus., Quality PB, 978-1-893361-44-7 **$16.99**

The Sacred Art of Lovingkindness: Preparing to Practice
By Rabbi Rami Shapiro; Foreword by Marcia Ford 5½ x 8½, 176 pp, Quality PB, 978-1-59473-151-8 **$16.99**

Thanking & Blessing—The Sacred Art: Spiritual Vitality through Gratefulness
By Jay Marshall, PhD; Foreword by Philip Gulley 5½ x 8½, 176 pp, Quality PB, 978-1-59473-231-7 **$16.99**

Writing—The Sacred Art: Beyond the Page to Spiritual Practice
By Rami Shapiro and Aaron Shapiro 5½ x 8½, 192 pp, Quality PB, 978-1-59473-372-7 **$16.99**

About SKYLIGHT PATHS Publishing

SkyLight Paths Publishing is creating a place where people of different spiritual traditions come together for challenge and inspiration, a place where we can help each other understand the mystery that lies at the heart of our existence.

Through spirituality, our religious beliefs are increasingly becoming a part of our lives—rather than *apart* from our lives. While many of us may be more interested than ever in spiritual growth, we may be less firmly planted in traditional religion. Yet, we do want to deepen our relationship to the sacred, to learn from our own as well as from other faith traditions, and to practice in new ways.

SkyLight Paths sees both believers and seekers as a community that increasingly transcends traditional boundaries of religion and denomination—people wanting to learn from each other, *walking together, finding the way.*

For your information and convenience, at the back of this book we have provided a list of other SkyLight Paths books you might find interesting and useful. They cover the following subjects:

Buddhism / Zen	Gnosticism	Poetry
Catholicism	Hinduism / Vedanta	Prayer
Chaplaincy		Religious Etiquette
Children's Books	Inspiration	Retirement & Later-Life Spirituality
Christianity	Islam / Sufism	
Comparative Religion	Judaism	Spiritual Biography
	Meditation	Spiritual Direction
Earth-Based Spirituality	Mindfulness	Spirituality
	Monasticism	Women's Interest
Enneagram	Mysticism	Worship
Global Spiritual Perspectives	Personal Growth	

Or phone, fax, mail or e-mail to: SKYLIGHT PATHS Publishing
Sunset Farm Offices, Route 4 • P.O. Box 237 • Woodstock, Vermont 05091
Tel: (802) 457-4000 • Fax: (802) 457-4004 • www.skylightpaths.com
Credit card orders: (800) 962-4544 (8:30AM–5:30PM EST Monday–Friday)
Generous discounts on quantity orders. SATISFACTION GUARANTEED. Prices subject to change.